Holy Herb
Marijuana Sacrament

Jeff Brown

Introduction: Ras Miguel Lorne
Preface: Ras Sekou S. Tafari

© Frontline Distribution Int'l Inc. & Miguel Lorne Publishers 2016
All Rights Reserved

No part of this publication may be reproduced, stored in a Retrieval system, or transmitted, in any form or by any means, Electronic, Mechanic, Photocopying, Recording, or otherwise, Without prior permission of FRONTLINE DISTRIBUTION INTERNATIONAL, INC & MIGUEL LORNE PUBLISHERS, Jamaica, Caribbean.

Library of Congress Control Number: 2009944091
ISBN #: 978-0-948390-27-2

2016 Edition Editor: Nastasia Grant-Terrier

Print Coordinator: Prizgar G.

Book Cover Design: Emani Alon & Ras Tzaddi Wadadah II

Table of Contents

Preface: Ras Sekou S. Tafari	i
Introduction: Ras Miguel Lorne	vi
Chapter 1: Offerings & Devotion	02
Chapter 2: The Use of Marijuana In Ancient Times	04
Chapter 3: Marijuana In Africa	07
Chapter 4: Marijuana In Ancient Egypt	09
Chapter 5: Marijuana In Ancient Iran	10
Chapter 6: Marijuana Use By The Moslems	11
Chapter 7: Marijuana In India	12
Chapter 8: Marijuana In China	17
Chapter 9: Marijuana In Japan	19
Chapter 10: Marijuana In Europe	20
Chapter 11: Marijuana In The New World	23
Chapter 12: Marijuana In Jamaica	28
Chapter 13: The Use of Marijuana as Incense	31
Chapter 14: The Israelite Use of Incense	36
Chapter 15: The Symbolism of Fire In The Ancient World	39
Chapter 16: Mysticism	40
Chapter 17: Marijuana as the Christian Sacrament	45
Chapter 18: Baptism	50
Chapter 19: The New Wine	59
Chapter 20: Inspiration	67
Chapter 21: Marijuana As The Eucharist	74
Chapter 22: Marijuana As The Tree of Life	76
Chapter 23: Revelations From Mt. Horeb	92
Chapter 24: The Sacramental Rights of Mankind	95
Chapter 25: Marijuana as the Only Peacemaker in This Generation	101
Chapter 26: Marijuana As a Medicine	103
Chapter 27: Marijuana As Food	105
Chapter 28: Why The Continuing Oppression	107
Chapter 29: An Introduction to the American Hemp Industry	122
Chapter 30: Thy Kingdom Come Oh Jah, Thy Rule Oh Negus I	125

Chapter 31: Governing the Ideal State by Marcus
               Mosiah Garvey National Hero   130
Chapter 32: God-Man & The Revelation of Jesus   138
Chapter 33: Man an Angel   142
Sources   143
Final Words   147
About The Author   148
Index   149

Preface: Ras Sekou Tafari

"Legalize The Herb!!"

The most hated, but yet the most loved plant on our planet, must be Cannabis, popularly known as Marijuana, and by many other common names, such as, *The Holy Herb* (The Hola Herb), Grass, Reefer, The Herb, Hemp, Colli (Kali), Hashish, Bhang, Pot, Ganja, The Holy Weed, Tampi, Bush, Mary Jane, Corn, Ily, Kush, Ta-Ma, Sensimella, Sess, Lambs Bread, and a host of other names, identifiable by countries, regions and peoples.

The Holy Herb is hated and targeted by governments and their agents, but loved by the masses of people, all over the world, who uses the plant in its most natural form, for many and varied reasons. There are at least three different species of this plant. They are as follows: (1) Cannabis Sativa, (2) Cannabis Indica, (3) Cannabis Ruberalis. Any of these three species can be used for Sacrament or medicinal purposes. Although, the first two species are the most popularly known of the three.

Humans have been using this herb for as long as time immemorial. Many ancient civilizations utilized this sacred plant, for multi reasons. Homer's Odyssey refers to it, as the herb that will make men leave their homes. In ancient Kemet, (Egypt) and other Nile Valley pre-historic civilizations, Cannabis usage was very prevalent amongst the elite. It was used by the Pharaohs who drank wines, beers, and teas processed from the hemp plant. It was also used to manufacture furniture, rope, clothing, shoes as well as to develop herbal tinctures, essential oils, for colds, fevers and other medical ailments. The high Priests and Priestesses also used it as incense along with Frankincense and Myrrh, which came from the Hinterlands of Punt, known today as Somalia.

The Priest and Priestesses would use this sacred herb to assist them in levitation, i.e. transforming oneself into a higher meditation.

Marijuana as a Sacrament has been a very ancient practice amongst all the nations of the world. It was used in Africa, Arabia, Persia, India, China, and even some parts of Europe, where it was imported from India and Afghanistan. It was also used by the native peoples of North, South and Central America regions, which included the Caribbean.

Its' use as a Sacrament, can still be found amongst many nations in the world. In the Congo region, in Central Africa, and other parts of Africa, some civilizations have been using it for thousands of years; and this is also the situation in India. The Hindus of India have been using this sacred plant, for over three thousand years or more, whilst paying homage to the Black Goddess — Kali. Some Sufis and Islamic Scholars also use it, to assist them in transforming themselves whilst in meditation. It is said, that according to Hadith that their great prophet Muhammad may have smoked *The Holy Herb* in the form of Hashish on various occasions.

Marijuana-Cannabis as a Sacrament, has been most popular in the 20th century until now, mainly amongst the Rastafari nation of Jamaica and the Caribbean. The Rastafari nation current concept of Cannabis usage is derived from using the Holy Herb to transform oneself into a higher spiritual realm very similar to ancient Kemet/Egypt.

The preparation of the dried leaves and flower-buds, are placed into a Chillum pipe; Steamer, or Kutche or rolled as a Spliff and smoked, to assist ones in acquiring a higher meditation, by levitating to become one with the Father and Mother principles, which take on the form of Haile Sellassie 1st and Empress Menen. Therefore, recreating the original concept of the Holy Trinity — Mother, Father and Child. As a Sacrament, marijuana takes the user into a peaceful state of mind, where one is at peace and perfect tranquility with one conscious self.

The practice of smoking from a Chillum pipe, Kutche or Steamer, can be witnessed at Nyahbinghi's celebrations, which are held to commemorate special occasions, that are relevant to the Rastafari nation. It is not unusual to see long stems of buds of the Holy Herb as part of the decoration of the Nyahbinghi tabernacle. Inside and outside of the tabernacle, the Rastafari faithful's can be seen smoking Spliffs, Chillums, Steamers, and other types of pipes and chalices. Spliffs are smoked by one person only – One man or woman to one Spliff, whilst chalices are shared collectively as Communion. The smoking of the Holy Herb continuously, is a great part of the celebration at Nyahbinghis or Groundations. The scent from the Ganja smoke can also be used similar to incense burning, since the *Holy Herb* has a very distinct aroma.

The founding father of the Rastafari nation — Leonard Percival Howell was a habitual smoker of the Holy Herb. It was

Howell who founded the first settlement of Rastafari on the Pinnacle Estate in Jamaica around 1939.

At Pinnacle, a lot of food crops were grown on the estate. However, Ganja or the Wisdom Weed was the main cash crop.

After chattel slavery was abolished in the British Caribbean in 1834, indentured servants from India were brought to the Caribbean to replace the Africans who were very resentful to continue working on the plantation. The bulk of the indentured laborers were sent to Trinidad, Guyana and Jamaica. The former two received the larger settlements of East Indians.

During this period of indentureship, and even up to the early 1960's, Cannabis was being imported from India by the British government for indentured servants to assist them with work and also for sacramental usage. *The Holy Herb* was imported in large quantities by Britain to their colony in Trinidad, to facilitate the large Hindu population that settled on the island, even after the period of indentureship was completed. The British Empire encouraged the smoking of marijuana by the East Indian population on the island for two reasons:

First reason, why the smoking and use of marijuana was sanctioned by the British, was for the use by those Hindus who honor the Goddess Kali; and secondly, as an encouragement to work steadily on the sugarcane and cocoa plantations. It was observed, that those who used the Holy Weed, were able to have a higher productivity level, as oppose to those who drank alcohol the night before, and were unproductive due to hangovers and thus, their level of productivity was at a low level compared to the smokers of Ganja.

We must salute the government of Jamaica for passing legislation on April 15, 2015, to decriminalize the usage of Ganja, and for securing the rights of the Rastafari nation dwelling on the island, the right to smoke or use Cannabis as a Sacrament, at least nineteen years after the first Ganja march and rally took place in Kingston, in 1996, led by the Rastafari nation to secure the rights to use the Holy Herb by the Faithfuls of the Rastafari Livity. The Rastafari nation, has been calling for the legalization of the *Holy Herb* as a Sacrament for over eighty years, on the island of Jamaica. However, Jamaica is the first country in the world where the use of marijuana is legal as a Sacrament.

It is about time, that the other Caribbean and world governments stop the senseless prohibition of this multipurpose herb plant. It is understandable, that there should be rules to govern its usage nonetheless, this herb should be free to be used by all world citizens eighteen years and over. Additionally, users should have the right to grow at least six plants for personal usage.

Cannabis is a herb. It should not be categorized as a drug. The majority of marijuana users can testify, that it is not a gateway drug, as falsely classified by President Reagan and the Federal Government. It is about time that the U.S. Supreme Court and the U.S Federal Government, legalize it's use, and strike it off from the books as an illicit drug.

Legalize the herb; and pay the millions of wrongly convicted citizens, who have been persecuted over the last seventy years with possession of a kilo or less, some substantial monetary reparation-compensation from the taxes on marijuana sales obtained from state and eventually federal operated dispensaries, across the United States. The same reparation-compensation formula should be adapted and implemented by the governments of other countries.

Many youths who obtained Cannabis felony convictions, were prevented or denied their right to reasonable employment, in corporate, state, or federal jobs in most countries.

When Ganja becomes legal, the law enforcement agencies can put more valuable time into apprehending the real hardcore criminals, including white-collar predators, and therefore prevent a large percentage of crimes from occurring.

According to a report in the Washington Post, of May 17th, 2016, "the Federal Government and most states are throwing away $28 Billion in yearly tax revenue by not legalizing marijuana, according to a new analysis from the tax foundation, an independent think tank."

In reading this book, the author Jeff Brown, a practicing Rastafari, from the Coptic House, gives us a poignant and refreshing history of Cannabis being used as a Sacrament, by various religions and spiritual orders. Whilst using scripture and oral traditional history to collaborate a powerful case for the legalization of Marijuana for Sacrament and other uses.

Read *The Holy Herb*, and get informed that Cannabis is a herb, and not a drug, used by many people across the world including the Rastafari nation as a Sacrament to find inner peace and tranquility as one desire, in ones heaven's.

Let's pay homage to our dear beloved brother — Peter Tosh who echoed in song over forty plus years ago, "... Legalize it." We should not beg or besiege any government for the moral right to legalize a natural and harmless plant. Free Up The Herb!!!

Ras Sekou S. Tafari

June 2016

The Struggle Continues!!!

Ready for Liberation!!!

Introduction: Ras Miguel Lorne

At this time in our History, there is a growing demand for the legislation of the Holy Herbs, referred to as Ganja, Marijuana, Dagga etc. The most hypocritical behavior of many societies manifests itself in their attitudes towards 'The Holy Herbs'. Many brothers and sisters have been "criminalized" and "stained for life" because of ganja related convictions.

We at Miguel Lorne Publishers have decided to put out this most valuable work as part of our support for the legislation of the Holy Herbs – Ganja. We are not, in any way, advocating wholescale, widespread, and uncontrolled use of marijuana, especially by young unsupervised teenagers, as we know of the possible harmful effects this may cause. However, we feel that if the entire issue is put on a table, above board, and is dealt with in a mature and responsible manner, that this will lessen hype, mystique, and magic which now surrounds the herbs and eventually lead to a reduction in the use and abuse of herbs.

It is an open secret that ganja is an important sacrament to the Rastafarian community world-wide. Yet, here in Jamaica, the root of Rastafari, evil continues to raise its ugly head by the pretenders in authority. In the recent Dennis Forsythe case, where he challenged the Government concerning his rights to use ganja in his religious observances, the Chief Justice, Lensley Wolfe showed up, not only his ignorance, but his hatred for Rastafarians, and a contempt for the natural people of the earth. Imagine a chief justice stating:

> "The enactments in the statute are not aimed against the practice by the participant (Forsythe) of his religion. He is free to practice his religion. The applicant's contention that he must be free to practice his religion unhindered is untenable. His understanding of the freedom of conscience is misguided. Taken to its logical conclusion, it would mean that the offering of human sacrifice in the practice of a religion would be unobjectionable."

The passage shows the level of ignorance and disrespect the Chief Justice holds for the African Race as there is no recorded history that Africans practiced human sacrifice. This is a thinking planted by the colonial masters in the minds of the house-slaves. Notice the pictures of the Ethiopian famines, not once did they ever show an Ethiopian eating another, despite extreme starvation.

Secondly, for the Chief Justice of a country, to liken an advocacy for the use of ganja to that of Cannibalism is low-class disrespect, whereby he should be fired from his office immediately. But because his appointment was not from the people, but by political lackeys, he can continue to disrespect I-n-I community despite our rich and consistent record on nation-building, along with our overwhelming contribution to the many areas of development of this country.

We have made the call on several occasions and will repeat it here, that Judges and Magistrates ought to be appointed by the people, and not by their political friends.

The irony of all this is that Britain, to which Jamaica's judiciary is subjected, as recent as September 1999, asked their judges to be lenient with cannabis users, who declare themselves Rastafarians, and that it should be treated as a "sacrament." Britain, a white country, with white judges is now showing greater respect to Rastafarians than Jamaica, a black country with "black judges."

We are of the view that the March of History cannot be stopped and it will just be a matter of time before ganja is legalized, Wolfe or no Wolfe.

Ras Miguel Lorne
1st August 2000

CHAPTER 1
"OFFERINGS OF DEVOTION"

"With offerings of devotion, ships from the isles will meet, to pour the wealth of nations and bring tribute to His feet."

The Coptic Church believes fully in the teachings of the Bible, and as such we have our daily oblations, and offer our sacrifices, made by fire unto our God with chants, psalms, and spiritual hymns, lifting up holy hands and making melody in our hearts.

Herb (marijuana) is a Godly creation from the beginning of the world. It is known as *the* 'Weed of Wisdom,' 'Angels' Food,' the 'Tree of Life' and even the 'Wicked Old Ganja Tree.' Its purpose in creation is a fiery sacrifice to be offered to our Redeemer during oblations.

The political organizations worldwide have framed mischief upon the Herb, and called it "drugs." To show that it is not a dangerous drug, let me inform my readers that it is used as food for mankind, and as a medicinal cure for diverse diseases.

Ganja is not for commerce; nevertheless, because of the oppression of the people, it was raised up as the only liberator of the people, and the sole peacemaker among the entire generation. Ganja is the sacramental rights of every man and woman worldwide, and we believe that any law against it – is only, the organized conspiracy of the United Nations and the political governments that assist in maintaining this conspiracy. The Coptic Church is not politically originated, and this was firmly expressed when we met with the political directorate of Jamaica during the period of pre-incorporation.

Seeing that religion, politics, and commerce are the three unclean spirits which separate the people from their God– we support no institution. Because of our non-political stand, the Church has received tremendous opposition from the politicians, who do not want the eyes of the people to be opened. Through its agency — the police force, our church has been severely harassed, victimized, and discriminated. Our members have passed through acts of police brutality: malicious destruction of legal properties, false imprisonment and disruption of divine services. All these atrocities performed upon the Church, under the name of political laws and their justice.

Walter Wells, Elder Priest of the

Holy Herb | Jeff Brown

Ethiopian Zion Coptic Church of Jamaica, West Indies

CHAPTER 2
"THE USE OF MARIJUANA IN ANCIENT TIMES"

Ancient and modern historians, archeologists, anthropologists, philologists, and the physical evidence they produce (artifacts, relics, textiles, cuneiform, languages, etc.) indicate that cannabis is one of mankind's oldest cultivated crops. The weaving of hemp fiber began 10,000 years ago, at approximately the same time as pottery making and prior to metal working. **(Columbia History of the World, Harper & Row, N.Y. 1981)**

Carl Sagan proposes evidence using the Bushmen of Africa to show hemp to have been the first plant cultivated by mankind, which dates back to the hunter-gatherer era. In his book "The Dragons of Eden," Carl Sagan has speculated that marijuana may have been the first crop planted by Stone Age Man, using the Pygmies as an example. The Pygmies were basically hunter-gatherers until they started planting the marijuana, which they use for religious purposes.

"Mircea Eliade, along with Sir James George Frazer (author of The Golden Bough), have both advocated the theory that early religions were derived from agricultural cults. In defense of the Pygmies, perhaps I should note that a friend of mine who has spent time with them says that for such activities as the patient stalking and hunting of mammals and fish, they prepare themselves through marijuana intoxication, which helps to make the long waits, boring to anyone further evolved than a Komodo dragon, at least moderately tolerable. Ganja is their only cultivation crop. It would be wryly interesting if in human history, the cultivation of marijuana led generally to the invention of agriculture, and thereby the civilization."

~ Carl Sagan ~

The use of marijuana is as old as the history of man and dates to the prehistoric period. Marijuana is closely connected with the history and development of some of the oldest nations on earth. It has played a significant role in the religions and cultures of Africa, the Middle East, India, and China.

Richard E. Schultes, a prominent researcher in the field of psychoactive plants, said in an article he wrote entitled "Man and Marijuana":

> *"Early man experimented with all plant materials that he could chew, and could not have avoided discovering the properties of cannabis (marijuana), for in his quest for seeds and oil, he certainly ate the sticky tops of the plant. Upon eating hemp, the euphoric, ecstatic and hallucinatory aspects may have introduced man to another worldly plane from which emerged religious beliefs, perhaps even the concept of deity. The plant became accepted as a special gift of the gods, a sacred medium for communion with the spiritual world and as such it has remained in some cultures to the present."*

The effects of marijuana were proof to the ancients that the spirit and power of the gods existed in this plant; it was literally a messenger (angel) or actually the flesh and blood, and/or the bread of the gods.

It was and continues to be a holy sacrament. Considered to be sacred, marijuana has been used in religious worship from before recorded history.

According to William A. Emboden Jr., in his book "Ritual Use of Cannabis Sativa L." pg. 235:

> *"Shamanistic traditions of great antiquity in Asia and the Near East had as one of their most important elements being the attempt to find God without a vale of tears; that Cannabis played a role in this, at least in some areas, is borne out in the philology surrounding the ritualistic use of the plant. Whereas Western religious traditions generally stress sin, repentance, and mortification of the flesh, certain older non-western religious cults seem to have employed Cannabis as a euphoriant, which allowed the participant a joyous path to the Ultimate; hence, such appellations as 'heavenly guide.'"*

According to "Licit and Illicit Drugs" by the Consumer Union, pg. 397-98:

> *"Ashurbanipal lived about 650 B.C., but the cuneiform descriptions of marijuana in his library 'are generally regarded as obvious copies of much older texts,' says Dr. Robert P. Walton, an American physician and authority on*

marijuana, *'This evidence serves to project the origin of hashish back to the earliest beginnings of history.'* "

(Ritual Use of Cannabis Sativa L., pg. 216):

"The earliest civilizations of Mesopotamia brewed intoxicating beer of more than 5,000 years ago; is it too much to assume that even earlier cultures experienced euphoria, accidently or deliberately, through inhalation of the resinous smoke of Cannabis?"

As a natural progression in our case, we will now give a short history of the religious use of marijuana in various cultures and countries of the world. The following information was taken from the most authoritative books dealing with the history of marijuana. They are listed in the back of this book.

CHAPTER 3
"MARIJUANA IN AFRICA"

The African continent is probably the zone showing the widest prevalence of the hemp drug habit. When white men first went to Africa, marijuana was a part of the native way of life.

Marijuana was also an integral part of religious ceremonies in the continent. The people utilized pipes and were observed inhaling the smoke from piles of smoldering hemp; some of these piles had been placed upon altars. The African dagga (marijuana) cults believed that Holy Cannabis was brought to earth by the gods.

Throughout the ancient world, Ethiopia was considered the home of the gods. It was referred to as the *Divine Land* and the *Land of Incense*. The Hashish of Ethiopia is superior to that of the Nile Delta; Soil, temperature, and humidity make a big difference.

The ancient Egyptians believed that they had received their divinities from Ethiopia and have always held to the ancient and honored tradition of their southern origin. Ethiopia is so important in history that it is mentioned as being in the Garden of Eden (Genesis 2:12).

The ancient Greek historian Diodorus Siculus wrote:

> *"The Ethiopians conceived themselves to be of greater antiquity than any other nation; and it is probable that, born under the sun's path, its warmth may have ripened them earlier than other men. They supposed themselves to be the inventors of worship, of festivals, of solemn assemblies of sacrifice, and every religious practice."*

> *"The earliest evidence for cannabis smoking in Africa outside of Egypt comes from fourteenth century Ethiopia, where two ceramic smoking-pipe bowls containing traces of cannabis were recently discovered during an archeological excavation. In many parts of East Africa, especially near Lake Victoria (the source of the Nile), hemp smoking and hashish snuffing cults still exist."*

The Bantus of Africa had secret "Dagga" cults, societies which restricted cannabis use to the ruling men. The Pygmies, Zulus, and Hottentots all used marijuana as medicine and a religious sacrament.

The "Dagga" cults, as mentioned earlier, believed Holy Cannabis was brought to earth by the Gods, particularly from the

"Two Dog Star" system that we call Sirius A and B. "Dagga" literally means "cannabis." Interestingly, the surviving Indo-European word for the plant can also be read as "canna," "reed" and "bi" means "two." Canna, as in "canine" and "bis," meaning two (bi) – "Two Dogs."

In South Central Africa, marijuana is held to be sacred and is connected with many religious and social customs. It is regarded by some sects as a magical plant possessing universal protection against all injuries to life, and is symbolic of peace and friendship; for this reason, certain tribes consider the usage of hemp a duty.

CHAPTER 4
"MARIJUANA IN ANCIENT EGYPT"

In the book, "Plants of the Gods: Origin of Hallucinogenic Use" by Richard E. Schultes and Albert Hofmann, (pg. 72), it is stated that specimens of marijuana nearly 4,000 years old have turned up in an Egyptian site, and in ancient Thebes the plant was made into a drink.

Thebes was the birthplace of Akhenaten (1,500 B.C.), the first monotheist. In El Amarna, the city of Akhenaten, archeologists have found hemp cordage.

CHAPTER 5
"MARIJUANA IN ANCIENT IRAN"

Ancient Iran was the source for the great Persian Empire. It is located slightly to the northeast of the ancient kingdoms of Sumeria, Babylonia, and Assyria.

According to Mircea Eliade, "Shamanic ecstasy induced by hemp smoke was known in ancient Iran." Professor Eliade has suggested that Zoroaster, the Persian prophet, said to have written the Zend-Avesta, was a user of hemp. In the Zend-Avesta, hemp occupies the first place on a list of 10,000 medicinal plants.

One of the few surviving books of the Zend-Avesta, called the Vendidad meaning *The Law Against Demons*, describes bhanga (marijuana) as Zoroaster's "good narcotic." The book also speaks of two mortals who were transported "in soul to the heavens" whereupon drinking from a cup of bhanga, they had the highest mysteries revealed to them. Professor Eliade has theorized that Zoroaster may have used hemp to bridge the metaphysical gap between heaven and earth.

The Zoroastrian priestly caste in ancient Media and Persia were also referred to as the Magi. The Magi were the pioneers of magnetism, science, and astrology. Thus, they predicted the coming of Christ and the "three Magi followed the star to Bethlehem." They brought incense, myrrh, and gold as gifts.

CHAPTER 6
"MARIJUANA USE BY THE MOSLEMS"

It is interesting to note that the use of hemp was not prohibited by Mohammed (570-632 A.D.) while the use of alcohol was. Moslems considered hemp a "Holy Plant" and medieval Arab doctors saw hemp as a sacred medicine which they called *Kannab*, among other names.

The Sufis (a Moslem sect) originating in the 8th century Persia used hashish as a means of stimulating mystical consciousness and the appreciation of the nature of Allah. To the Sufis, the eating of hashish was "an act of worship." They maintained that hashish gave them otherwise unattainable insights into themselves: a deeper understanding which made them feel witty, gave happiness, reduced anxiety and worry, and increased musical appreciation.

According to one Arab legend, Haydar, the Persian founder of the religious order of Sufi came across the cannabis plant while wandering in the Persian mountains. Usually a reserved and silent man, when he returned to his monastery after eating some cannabis leaves, his disciples were amazed at how talkative and animated (full of spirit) he seemed. After cajoling Haydar into telling them what he had done to make him feel happy, his disciples went out into the mountains and tried the cannabis for themselves. So it was, according to the legend, the Sufis came to know the pleasures of hashish. (Taken from the introduction to *A Comprehensive Guide to Cannabis Literature* by Ernest L. Abel.)

"God has granted you the privilege of knowing the secret of these leaves. Thus when you eat it, your dense worries may disappear and your exalted minds may become polished."

~ Abu Khalid, 632 A.D. ~

CHAPTER 7
"MARIJUANA IN INDIA"

In Indian tradition, marijuana is associated with immortality. There is a complex myth of the churning of the Ocean of Milk by the gods; their joint act of creation. They were in search of Amrita, the elixir of eternal life. When the gods, helped by demons, churned the ocean to obtain Amrita, one of the resulting nectars was cannabis. After churning the ocean, the demons attempted to gain control of Amrita (marijuana), but the gods were able to prevent this seizure, giving cannabis the name Vijaya "victory" to commemorate their success.

Other ancient Indian names for marijuana were *sacred grass, hero leaves, joy, rejoicer, desired in the three worlds, gods' food, fountain of pleasures* and *Shiva's plant*.

Early Indian legends maintained that the angel of mankind lived in the leaves of the marijuana plant. It was so sacred that it was reputed to deter evil and cleansed its user of sin. In Hindu mythology hemp is a holy plant given to man for the "welfare of mankind" and is considered to be one of the divine nectars able to give man anything: from good health to long life, to visions of the gods. Nectar is defined as the fabled drink of the gods.

Tradition maintains that when nectar or Amrita dropped from heaven cannabis sprouted from it. In Hindu mythology, Amrita means immortality; also, the ambrosial drink which it produced. In India, hemp is made into a drink and is reputed to be the favorite drink of Indra (the King of the Indian gods). Tradition shows that the god, Indra, gave marijuana to the people so that they might attain elevated states of consciousness, delight in worldly joy, and freedom from fear.

According to Hindu legends, Shiva, the Supreme God of many Hindu sects had some family squabble and went off to the fields. He sat under a hemp plant so as to be sheltered from the heat of the Sun; he happened to eat some of its leaves. He felt so refreshed from the hemp plant that it became his favorite food, and that is how he got his title, the Lord of Bhang (an Indian hemp beverage) (Bang/la/desh=Hemp/hill/people).

Cannabis is mentioned as a medicinal and magical plant as well as the "sacred grass" in the Atharvaveda (dated 2000-1400 B.C.). It also calls hemp one of five kingdoms of herbs... which release us from anxiety, and refers to hemp as a "source of happiness," "joy-giver" and "liberator." Although the holy book, the Shastras, forbids the worship of the plant, it has been venerated and used as a sacrifice to the deities.

Indian tradition, writing and belief is that "Siddhartha" (the Buddha), used and ate nothing but hemp and its seeds for six years prior to announcing (discovering) his truths and becoming the Buddha.

Cannabis held a pre-eminent place in the Tantric religion which evolved in Tibet in the Seventh century A.D. Tantrism was a religion based on fear of demons. To combat the demonic threat to the world, the people sought protection in plants such as cannabis which were set afire to overcome evil forces.

In the tenth century A.D., hemp was extolled as *Indracanne*, the "food of the gods." A fifteenth-century document refers to cannabis as "light-hearted," "joy-full," "astringency," "heat," "speech-giving," "inspiration of mental powers," "excitability" and the capacity to remove wind and phlegm.

Indian medical works dating back to 1300 A.D. list among the effects of cannabis: it sharpens the memory, sharpens the wits, creates energy, stimulates mental powers and is an elixir vitae.

Indian Commission witnesses testified that cannabis is "refreshing and stimulating, alleviates fatigue, creates the capacity for hard work and the ability to concentrate, and gives rise to pleasurable sensations, that one is at peace with everybody." (Great Britain 1969: 174-175, 191-192). In essence, Moslems, as well as Hindus, share the belief that ganja is a holy plant. (Chopra 1969: 216-218).

Today, in Tantric Buddhism of the Himalayas of Tibet, cannabis plays a very significant role in the meditative ritual to facilitate deep meditation and heighten awareness. In modern India, it is taken at Hindu and Sikh temples and Mohammedan shrines. Among fakirs (Hindu ascetics), bhang is associated with the divine spirit.

> *"In their references to the use of bhang, the Brahmins were matter-of-fact rather than lyrical, 'It gives good bhakti,' said Shankar Lal: 'You get a very good bhakti with bhang.' He went on to define bhakti as the sort of devotional act which consists in emptying the mind of all worldly distractions and thinking only of God. The*

'arrived' devotee is able to keep his thoughts from straying off onto trivial or lustful topics; in his impersonal trance he becomes oblivious to mundane concerns..."

~ *The Marijuana Papers by David Solomon (P.74)* ~

Cannabis is offered to Shiva during temple worship on Shivaratri day as "food of the gods" (Hasan 1974). Cannabis is used in worship and in offerings made in the fulfillment of vows; similarly, bhang is customarily served at weddings and at religious festivals (Great Britain 1969: 159-165).

At the turn of the twentieth century, the report of the Indian Hemp Drugs Commission, set up to study the use of hemp in India contains the following:

"It is inevitable that temperaments would be found to whom the quickening spirit of bhang is the spirit freedom and knowledge. In the ecstasy of bhang, the spark of the Eternal in man turns into light the murkiness of matter."

The Vedas, the most ancient Hindu writings, are full of praise for a plant or drug called Soma, which was said to cure a variety of diseases and enable the practiced yogi to see God face-to-face. Dr. Michael R. Aldrich, the most erudite of all historians of cannabis, believes that Soma was some form of cannabis drug.

"Bhang is the Joy-giver, the Sky-flyer, the Heavenly-Guide, the Poor Man's Heaven, the Soother of Grief...No god or man is as good as the religious drinker of bhang...The supporting power of bhang has brought many a Hindu family safe through the miseries of famine. To forbid or even seriously to restrict the use of so gracious a herb as the hemp would cause widespread suffering and annoyance; and to large bands of worshipped ascetics, deep- seated anger.

"It would rob the people of a solace in discomfort, of a cure in sickness, of a guardian whose gracious protection saves them from the attacks of evil influences, and whose mighty power makes the devotee of the Victorious, overcoming the demons of hunger and thirst, of panic, fear, of the glamour of Maya or matter, and of madness, able in rest to brood on the Eternal, till the Eternal, possessing him body and soul, frees him from the haunting of self and receives him into the Ocean of Being. "These beliefs the

Musalman devotee shares to the full. Like his Hindu brother, the Musalman fakir reveres bhang as the lengthener of life, the freer from the bonds of self. Bhang brings union with the Divine Spirit. 'We drank bhang and the mystery I am He grew plain.'"

Much of the holiness of bhang (marijuana) is due to its virtues of clearing the head and stimulating the brain to thought. Among ascetics, the sect known as Atits is especially devoted to hemp. No social or religious gathering of Atits is complete without the use of the hemp plant; smoked in ganja or drunk in bhang. To its devotee, bhang is an ordinary plant that became holy from its guardian and healing qualities.

According to one account, when nectar was produced from the churning of the ocean, something was wanted to purify the nectar. The deity Mahadev supplied the want of a nectar-cleanser by creating bhang. This bhang Mahadev made from his own body, and so, it is called angai or body-born (body and blood of the Lord).

According to another account, some nectar dropped to the ground and from the ground, the bhang plant sprang. It was because they used this child of nectar or of Mahadev in agreement with religious forms, that the seers or Rishis became Siddha, or one with the deity.

"He who, despite the example of the Rishis uses no bhang, Shall lose his happiness in this life and in the life to come. In the end he shall be cast into hell. The mere sight of bhang cleans from as much as a thousand horse-sacrifices or a thousand pilgrimages. He who scandalizes the user of bhang shall suffer the torments of hell so long as the sun endures."

"He who drinks bhang foolishly or for pleasure without religious rites is as guilty as the sinner of sins. He who drinks wisely and according to rule, be he ever so low, even though his body is smeared with human ordure and urine, is Shiva (a man of god). No god or man is as good as the religious drinker of bhang."

The students of the scriptures at Benares are given bhang before they sit to study. At Benares, students of the Ujjain and other holy yogis, bairagis and sanyasis take deep drafts of bhang that they may center their thoughts on the Eternal.

To bring back to reason an unhinged mind, the best and cleanest bhang leaves should be boiled in milk and turned to clarified butter. Salamisri, saffron, and sugar should be added, and completely eaten. Besides, over the demons of madness, bhang is vijaya (victorious) over the demons of hunger and thirst. By the help of bhang, ascetics pass days without food or drink.

CHAPTER 8
"MARIJUANA IN CHINA"

In China cannabis has been called "Ta-Ma" or "great-hemp" to differentiate it from the minor fiber plants. The Chinese pictogram for true hemp is a large "man," indicating the strong relationship between man and hemp.

Hemp was so highly regarded in ancient China that the Chinese called their country "The Land of Mulberry and Hemp." Hemp was a symbol of power over evil and in Emperor Shen Nung's pharmacopeia it was known as the "liberator of sin."

The Chinese believed that the legendary Shen Nung first taught of hemp in the 28th B.C., Shen Nung is credited with developing the science of medicine from the curative powers of plants. So highly regarded was Shen Nung that he was deified. Today, he is regarded as the father of Chinese medicine and the Lord of fire. He sacrificed on Tai Shan, a mountain of hoary antiquity.

A statement in the Pen-Tsao Ching, which seems to be of some significance: "[Cannabis] grows along rivers and valleys at Tai Shan, but it is now common everywhere." Mount Tai is in Shantung Province, where the cultivation of the hemp plant is still intensive to this day. Whether this early attribution indicates the actual geographic origin of the cultivation of the Cannabis plant remains to be seen. (*An Archaeological and Historical Account Cannabis in China* by **Hui-Lin Li**)

A Chinese Taoist priest wrote in the fifth century B.C. that cannabis was used in combination with Ginseng to set forward time in order to reveal future events. It is recorded that the Taoist recommended the addition of cannabis to their incense burners in the 1st century A.D., and the effects thus produced were highly regarded as a means of achieving immortality. In early Chinese Taoist ritual, the fumes and odors of incense burners were said to have produced a mystic exaltation and contribution to well-being.

Webster's *New Riverside Dictionary* defines marijuana: 1. Hemp: 2. The dried flower clusters and leaves of the hemp plant, esp. when taken to induce euphoria. Euphoria is defined as a strong feeling of elation or well-being.

One of the later Chinese names meant "delight giver." A fourth- century report asserts that eating hemp causes the user to see spirits, and several hundred years later the Chinese were taking

Cannabis for the "enjoyment of life." (*Man and Marijuana* - Richard E. Schultes)

Like the practice of medicine around the world, early Chinese doctoring was based on the concept of demons. The only way to cure the sick was to drive out the demons. The early priest doctors used marijuana stalks, into which snake-like figures were carved. Standing over the body of the stricken patient, his cannabis stalk poised to strike, the priest pounded the bed and commanded the demon to be gone. The cannabis stalk with the snake carved on it (the staff with entwined serpents) was the forerunner to the sign of modern medicine.

The Chinese utilized all parts of the plant for medicine. The flowers are used in treating open wounds; the seed coat and its adhering resin are used to stimulate the nervous System; the seeds themselves are used to counteract inflammations and skin irritations and are considered tonic, (mentally or morally invigorating—Webster's 2nd definition); a restorative of good health; laxative and diuretic and excellent for worming babies and animals. The oil is used as a hair tonic and to counteract sulfur poisoning; the fresh juice of the leaves is used for treating scorpion bites and the ash obtained after burning the plant is used in sky rockets. (From: *The Cultivator's Handbook of Marijuana* by Bill Drake, 1970.)

CHAPTER 9
"MARIJUANA IN JAPAN"

Hemp was used in ancient Japan in ceremonial purification rites and for driving away evil spirits. In Japan, Shinto priests used a gohei, a short stick, with undyed hemp fibers (for purity) attached to one end.

According to Shinto beliefs, evil and impurity cannot exist alongside one another, and so by waving the gohei (purity) above someone's head, the evil spirit inside him would be driven away. Clothes made of hemp were especially worn during formal and religious ceremonies because of hemp's traditional association with purity.

CHAPTER 10
"MARIJUANA IN EUROPE"

According to Nikolaas J. van der Merwe (Department of Archaeology, University of Cape Town, South Africa) the peasants of Europe have been using cannabis as ritual material, and to smoke or chew as far back as oral traditions go.

Marijuana was an integral part of the Scythian cult of the dead wherein homage was paid to the memory of their departed leaders. This use of cannabis was found in frozen Scythian tombs dated from 500 to 300 B.C.

Along with the cannabis, a miniature tripod-like tent over a copper censer was found in which the sacred plant was burned.

It is interesting to note that two extraordinary rugs were also found in the frozen Scythian tombs. One rug had a border frieze with a repeated composition of a horseman approaching the Great Goddess who holds the "Tree of Life" in one hand and raises the other hand in welcome.

In a famous passage written in about 450 B.C., Herodotus describes the funeral rites that took place when a king died among the Scythians—a nomadic tribe that roamed the steps from Turkestan to Siberia. After the burial, he wrote, the Scythians would purify themselves by setting up small tepee-like structures covered by rugs which they would enter to inhale the fumes of hemp seeds thrown onto red-hot Stones. "It smolders and sends forth such billows of smoke that no Greek steambath could surpass it," commented Herodotus, "The Scythians howl with pleasure at these baths."

During the Roman Empire, Galen, writing in the second century A.D., notes that this herb was often passed around at banquets to promote hilarity and joy. Some hashish still said to be potent, was recently found in an airtight container in the wreck of a Carthaginian warship thought to have been sunk in the Second Punic War (218-201 B.C.) off the coast of Sicily.

The date on which marijuana was introduced into Western Europe is not known, but it must have been very early. An urn containing marijuana leaves and seeds, unearthed near Berlin, Germany, are believed to date from 500 B.C.

According to Professors Graeme Whittington and Jack Jarvis of the University of St. Andrews in Fife, Scotland, hemp was grown agriculturally in tenth century Scotland. Sediment from Kilconquhar Loch, near Fife, had cannabis pollen. Cannabis from around the same time has been found in East Anglia, Wales, and in Finland. The hemp was found to have been grown in areas occupied by religious groups of the time. Jarvis commented in an Omni interview, "...the decline of these ecclesiastical establishments may have coincided with a decline in the growing of hemp."

In 16th century Europe, Benedictine monk and qualified bachelor of medicine, Francois Rabelais (1494-1553) was persecuted by religious and civil authorities for the release of his books Gargantua& Pantagruel. The author claimed that secret knowledge could be found by the studying of this book. In the book "Pantagruel," Rabelais gives a distinct description of hemp, which he referred to as 'The Herb Pantagruelion':

> *"The leaves sprout out all round the stalk at equal distances, to the number of five or seven at each level; and it is by special favor of nature that they are grouped in these two odd numbers, which are both divine and mysterious. The scent is strong, and unpleasant to delicate nostrils."*

Rabelais goes on to describe unmistakable usages of hemp:

> *"All the cotton plants of Tylos on the Persian Gulf, of Arabia, and of Malta have not dressed so many people as this plant alone. It protects armies against cold rain, much more effectively than did the skin tents of old. It protects theatres and amphitheaters against the heat; it is hung around woods and coppices for the pleasure of hunters; it is dropped onto sweat water and sea water for the profit of fishermen. It shapes and makes serviceable boots, high boots, leggings, shoes, pumps, slippers, and nailed shoes. By it bows are strung, arbalests bent, and slings made."*

Rabelais ends a chapter devoted to the herb Pantagruelion with the following mysterious message:

> *"And marry our Goddesses; which is their one means of rising to be gods. In the end, they decided to deliberate*

on a means of preventing this and called a council."

What Rabelais is referring to by "marry our goddesses" is the spiritual marriage with one's *higher self*. This imagery is used often in Gnostic and Zoroastrian literature. The last sentence of the chapter could very well refer to the formation of the politically motivated Roman Catholic Church when sects like the Gnostics and Essenes were driven underground or wiped out. It is at this time when the sacrament disappeared from the script! And this is echoed in Timothy 4:3-5, in the New Testament: "*Forbidding certain marriages and commanding to abstain from meats which God hath created to be received with thanksgiving of them which believe and know the truth.*" Genesis 1 refers to meat as herbs and the seeds of herbs.

By the middle of the nineteenth century, the medicinal uses of cannabinols passed from Europe to North America. Many Cannabis preparations were available at the corner drugstore. In 1857, Fitz Hugh Ludlow acquired a tincture of the Indica variety while living in Poughkeepsie, New York. He paid six cents a dose for it in the form of "Tilden's Extract." Ludlow, then only 16 and with his imagination enflamed by THE THOUSAND AND ONE NIGHTS, declared hemp "the drug of the traveler," which allowed him to journey mentally around the globe, as well as, into the higher more mystic regions. His experience eventually led him to write *The Hasheesh Eater*, America's first native contribution to the literature on hemp highs.

CHAPTER 11
"MARIJUANA IN THE NEW WORLD"

According to Richard L. Lingeman in his book *Drugs from A to Z*, page 146, "Marijuana smoking was known by the Indians before Columbus."

After the Spanish conquest in 1521, the Spaniards recorded that the Aztecs (Mayans) used marijuana. The book *The Great American Hemp Industry* by Jack Frazier has references about the pre-Columbian usage of hemp in the Americas. His book is not copyrighted; nonetheless, he has given permission for the usage of anything from the book.

***The Great American Hemp Industry* by Jack Frazier 1991 Solar Age Press Box 610 Peterstown, WV 24963:**

Sections "Hemp Discovers America" and "The Sea people":

"The earliest report of wild hemp in North America is from an expedition to Virginia in 1524 by John De Verrazzano, a Florentine, sailing under a French flag. Jacques Cartier, the French explorer, made three voyages to Canada: in 1535, 1536, and 1541. He reported seeing hemp on all three occasions. When Richard Hakluyt compiled his classic "Divers Voyages Touching the Discovery of America" in 1582, he included hemp in a list of plants found growing in North America."

"There is enough evidence to indicate that marijuana was already in the New World when Columbus discovered America. There is also evidence indicating that America had contact with Old World Civilizations long before Columbus. With hemp being such an important plant in the Old World, it undoubtedly was passed on. Some of the main items of trade in ancient times were herbs, spices, incense, wines, and smoking mixtures."

"Gordon, Heyerdahl, Charles Hapgood, George Carter and others have been trying for years to tell us that there were numerous contacts between the Mediterranean and America and Asia long before Columbus, going back to the first papyrus boat voyages from Africa by the Phoenicians and Egyptians. Thor Heyerdahl even built a reed boat and sailed it to the Americas to prove it was possible."

"Other evidence is in the form of pre-Columbian maps, such as the PIRI REIS map from Egypt showing the coastline of Antarctica - without ice; Roman and Hebrew coins from several locations in Tennessee and Kentucky; Phoenician, Hebrew, and Minoan inscriptions elsewhere in the southeast. The Greek classics reveal that the Phoenicians, who gave us our alphabet, made several voyages to the Americas. In South and Central America, Gordon cites evidence of an even more convincing nature; sculptured heads of Africans, Romans, Hebrews and Chinese from early B.C. periods; more Roman and Phoenician coins and inscriptions and pre-Columbian literature of the Mayan culture. (Frazier quoting Cyrus Gordon's Before Columbus: Links Between the Old World and Ancient America [N.Y., 19711, pp. 46-49, 170-177])."

"One reason it has taken so long to unravel early American history is due to the destruction of the Mayan libraries by the Spaniard, Diego de Landa, who ordered the destruction, and said, 'Among the Maya we found a great number of books written with their characters, and because they contained nothing but superstitions and falsehoods about the Devil, we burned them all; which the Indians felt most deeply and over which they showed much sorrow.'"

"The authentic history of the wars against the American Indians is one of the bloodiest sagas in recorded history. It seems to be a common characteristic of cultural imperialism to attempt the complete elimination of all traces of the native culture by the invading culture. There has been much cultural genocide throughout history. Much of history as a consequence has been lost or altered. The Roman Catholic Church had the Inquisition and anyone or anything that did not conform to its dogma was brutally suppressed. During this period known as the Dark Ages, history was written to justify the actions of the White Europeans Catholics and later the White European Protestants."

Section entitled: Pipes, Bowls, and Joints

"We know from archeological discoveries that stone pipes were used ritually in the ancient Near East; such

pipes consist of a bowl and stem carved out of one stone. Some have animal heads on the bowl, and some have a hand (with all five fingers) carved in relief on the bottom of the bowl."

"It is interesting," says Gordon, "to note that American Indian pipes sometimes have animal heads carved on the bowl, as well as hands with all five fingers carved beneath the bowl. The heads indicate that the bowls were personified, while the hands not only suggest that the fragrant smoke was being offered, but also that the whole cultic object was called a hand [kaf - hand is the name of such an object in Hebrew]."

"Since such smoking bowls appear during Old Testament times in the Near East, it is possible that the American peace pipes are an adaptation of Near East kaf pipes. They could have been introduced by the Canaanites like those who reached America in 531 B.C. or by later visitors like the Mediterranean merchant prince of about A.D. 300 from Iximche in the Guatemalan province of Chimaltenango. (**Cyrus Gordon, Before Columbus: Links Between the Old World and Ancient America [N.Y. 1971 pp. 1421]**). Most Indian tribes used the pipe only for ceremonial purposes, smoking was not a habit, but a ritual."

"Historical and archeological evidence seems to indicate the marijuana cigarette or joint originated somewhere in Mexico, Central America, or the Island of Hispaniola (Haiti). One of the early reports from the Caribbean of 1561 sounds suspiciously like an early version of the cigarette. Most historians have assumed, wrongly I think, that the writer was talking about the tobacco plant."

"In this island, as in some other provinces of these countries, there are certain bushes, not very large, like reeds, which produce a leaf like that of the walnut (authors note: Anyone that has seen a walnut leaf must agree that it resembles hemp), but a little larger, which is held in high estimation by the people of the country where it is used, and very much prized by the slaves which the Spaniards brought from Ethiopia."

(Note that the slaves came from Ethiopia [the ancient name

of Africa] and readily took to the herb. It was the descendants of these same slaves that went on to found the Ethiopian Zion Coptic Church in Jamaica).

The unabridged Webster's Third New International Dictionary includes as its first definition of marijuana: A wild tobacco — (Nicotiana Glauca).

There are reports of awestruck Englishmen who saw Indians sitting in council and passing the "Peace Pipe" from one chief to the next. When asked by an inquisitive white man, "What is in the pipe?" they said, "The sacrament of the Father Creator."

On page 16 of Spare Time Magazine, Aug. 28, 1985, an article by Judi Martin on the excavation site of a 500-year old Indian village in Ontario, Canada:

> *"Among the collection of artifacts taken from the Morrison Dig site are stone and ceramic smoking pipes which contained traces of hemp and tobacco that is five times stronger than the cigarettes smoked today.*
>
> *"When the Spanish "discovered" Mexico in the 1500's they found the Aztecs smoking a reed type cigarette. The Aztecs were famous for their "perfumed" reed cigarettes. It wasn't until the 1890's that an American archeologist discovered what they were. Dr. Walter Fewkes, in his investigations of the Hopi of New Mexico, found what answers completely described [hemp] as being used by the Mexicans.*
>
> *"These cigarettes are found in large numbers in the sacrificial caves in the vicinity, and appear to be a survival of one of the most primitive of smoking arrangements. The natives of Mexico are found with a weed called Marijuana, for mixing with the tobacco in their cigarettes, and when it is smoked and inhaled by them, is said to produce a hilarious spirit in the smoker."*
> **(J.D. McGuire, Report of National Museum (Wash., 1871).)**

According to *The Marijuana Papers* by David Solomon, Book Three, Ch. 8., Cannabis: A Reference, Dr. William H. McGlothlin, Ph.D., Harvard— "Marijuana plays a role in certain primitive

South American tribe. The present day Kuna Indians of Panama use marijuana as a sacred herb and the Cora Indians of the Sierra Madre Occidental of Mexico smoke marijuana in the course of their sacred ceremonies."

In the *Ritual Use of Cannabis Sativa L.* by William A. Emboden, Jr., pages 229 and 231, is the following:

> "A particularly interesting account of a Tepehua (no relationship to "Tepecana") Indian ceremony with cannabis was published in 1963 by the Mexican ethnologist Roberto William Garcia of the University Of Veracru4 Mexico. The Tepehua linguistically and culturally belonged to the Totonac of Veracruz, northernmost branch of the Maya language family."

> "In his account of Tepehua religion and ritual, William Garcia (1963: 215-21) describes in some detail a communal curing ceremony focused on a plant called Santa Rose, 'The Herb Which Makes One Speak', which he identified botanically as Cannabis Sativa. According to Garcia, it is worshipped as an earth deity and is thought to be alive and comparable to a piece of the heart of God. (Body and blood)"

In 1890, Carl Lumholtz, a Swiss ethnologist, studied many of the Tribes in the Sierra Madre Del Norte. He discovered that the Tepecano often substituted Marijuana for Peyote. The Tepecano always kept their cannabis in votive bowls or in niches together with cotton balls. The cotton symbolized rain clouds which were the ultimate blessing to the Indians. The cannabis absorbed the nature of the clouds and the use of it became a prayer for rain (blessings).

The Lipan Apache are known to use cannabis in their ceremonial breakfast.

CHAPTER 12
"MARIJUANA IN JAMAICA"

According to Jamaican folk beliefs, Ganja has a divine origin. It is the source of "wisdom" and "peace"; its use is both sacred and secular.

Some tradition maintains that it was the Arawak Indians who first used ganja in Jamaica. These Indians were known for their peacefulness and were completely wiped out by persecution, slavery and disease brought by the Spanish invaders and later the English. They both used the Bible to justify their trade in human flesh, saying that they were going to *civilize the savages*. Catholic and Protestant nations were both involved in this genocide as well as in the slave trade from Africa.

In 1979, Dennis Forsythe, PhD., presented a report to the department of sociology at the University of the West Indies, Jamaica.

Here is part of that report:

"Rastas come together around the usage of Ganja, which they use for smoking, eating, drinking, sniffing and massaging. For them, Ganja is not a drug, but a 'Holy' herb. So omnipotent is the ingredient of their culture and so positive is their estimation of its value to man, that they call it the 'wisdom weed' and the 'spiritual meat' of the movement. Symbolically, Herb for Rastas grew out of the grave of King Solomon, and because of its wholesome effects, has the power to 'heal the nation' by bringing every man to the self-knowledge appropriate and fitting for 'Ever-living Life.'

"The Ethiopian Zion Coptic Church (with chapters in Jamaica and Miami) reveres Ganja as their 'Holy' Eucharist and 'spiritual intensifier' with Biblical, historical and divine associations. Biblical justification for its usage is found on the first page of the Bible (Genesis 1 vs. 29). For the Brethren, ganja is the mystical body and blood of Jesus' — the burnt offering unto God made by fire — which allows a member to see and know the 'living God' or the 'God in Man'. Presently, the Ethiopian Zion Coptic organization is fighting to get U.S. officials, as well as the Jamaican Government, to 'free up' the plant on religious grounds. They derive their moral authority to use the herbs

from their personal experiences with the plant and also from the Book of Genesis which approved the usage of 'every herb bearing seed'.

"Rastas, through the usage of Ganja, feel themselves to be divinely inspired; experiencing the same magnificence of spirit and oneness with nature which Moses must have experienced 'high' on the mountain top in the form of the 'burning bush'(herbs), as did Jesus 'high' on top of Mount Sinai.

"Every Rastaman has experience, to varying degrees, the wholesome effects of herbs. They talk of this all the time. That is the only reason for using it."

Barbara Blake Hannah, a Jamaican journalist, wrote a book entitled "Rastafari - The New Creation." In one of the chapters entitled "The Holy Herb" is the following:

"Herb smoking enhances intellectual powers; it can speed up thinking on one particular subject, isolate those thoughts from everyday reality, and place the user in a world of his own, rather than the society in which he must function. This, at the same time, does not remove the user from the midst of reality — thus enabling him to function on three levels of existence at once: physical, mental, and spiritual."

The following article entitled *"Eye Spy,"* and written by Garry Hamilton, was taken from **NEXUS** magazine:

"Among most mariners, the thought of setting sail through treacherous, reef-ridden waters at night without light or compass inspires only dread. But Jamaican fishermen regularly do just that after fortifying themselves with marijuana steeped in white rum. The evil weed, they say, sharpens their night vision - a claim supported by new research from American ophthalmologist Albert Lockhart and Jamaican pharmacologist Manley West.

"Lockhart first became interested in marijuana's medicinal powers after observing the low incidence of the eye disease glaucoma among Rastafarians, members of a religion long known for its association with Cannabis. After testing volunteers at the University of the West

Indies, in Kingston, Jamaica, Lockhart and West found that marijuana did indeed lower intraocular pressure, the main cause of glaucoma. Impressed, the two researchers set to work isolating the compound responsible for the effect and named their discovery Canasol.

"Lockhart, Who runs a private practice in Dallas, Texas, and prescribes the marijuana derivative to his patients, has since documented yet another benefit. 'When we give medication to a patient, we always ask what effect they experience after taking it,' he says. 'And with Canasol, they always say their night vision improves.'

"Just how the substance helps humans see better in the dark is still unknown, and Lockhart says that a lack of outside interest in marijuana is partly to blame for the dearth of research. 'The historical literature is full of records describing how people have used marijuana for various reasons,' he says, 'We know it has a wide range of medicinal potentials, but North Americans don't seem to understand this. They think that because a compound comes from something illegal, it must be bad.'"

CHAPTER 13
"THE USE OF MARIJUANA AS INCENSE"

In the temples of the ancient world, the main sacrifice was the inhalation of incense. Incense is defined as the perfume or smoke from spices and gums when burned in celebrating religious rites or as an offering to a deity. Bronze and gold incense burners were cast very early in history and their forms were often inspired by cosmological themes representing the harmonious nature of the universe.

It was said that Moses, at the direction of Almighty God, first brought in the use of incense in public worship, and the other nations of antiquity copied the practice from him. It was, however, a practice that began with Adam.

The "**Book of Jubilees**," an Apocryphal book, (the Apocrypha was considered canonical by the early church and is to this day by the Ethiopian Zion Coptic Church) states that, *"on the day when Adam went forth from the Garden of Eden, he offered as a sweet savour an offering of frankincense, galbanum, stacte, and spices, in the morning with the rising of the sun, from the dry when he covered his shame."*

And of Enoch we read, *"he burnt the incense of the sanctuary, even sweet spices, acceptable before the Lord, on the Mount."* Ethiopia was known by the Egyptians and others as the "sacred land" and "the land of incense."

From *Tales of Hashish* / **Francois Lallemand (Pg.117):**

"Scientists from the Egyptian Expedition were of the opinion that hashish was nothing other than our hemp plant, whose properties are weakened in the north, and what seems to confirm that theory is the superiority of the hashish of Abyssinia (Ethiopia) over that of the Nile Delta. We know how much soil, temperature, humidity, and cultivation can change the appearance, and especially the properties of plants." **Napoleon's Egyptian Expedition (1798 - 1799).**

According to Encyclopedia Britannica: the section on "Pharmacological Cults":

"The ceremonial use of incense in contemporary ritual is most likely a relic of the time when the psychoactive properties of incense brought the ancient worshipper into touch with supernatural forces."

The following piece was taken from "Licit and Illicit Drugs" (pg. 31):

"In the Judaic world, the vapors from burnt spices and aromatic gums were considered part of the pleasurable act of worship. In Proverbs (27:9) it is said that 'ointment and perfumes rejoice the heart.'

"Perfumes were widely used in Egyptian worship. Stone altars have been unearthed in Babylon and Palestine, which have been used for burning incense made of aromatic wood and spices. While the casual readers today may interpret such practices as mere satisfaction of the desire for pleasant odors, this is almost certainly an error, in many or most cases, a psychoactive drug was being inhaled.

"In the islands of the Mediterranean 2,500 years ago and in Africa hundreds of years ago, for example, leaves and flowers of a particular plant were often thrown upon bonfires and the smoke inhaled; the plant was marijuana. (1-Edward Preble and Gabriel V. Laurey, "Plastic Cement: The Ten Cent Hallucinogen," International Journal of the Addictions, 2-Fall 2967:271-272).

According to the book "The Great American Hemp Industry," Pipe Bowls found in Palestine and Syria dating 1000 to 600 B.C. match an illustration from National Geographic April 91' showing Ramses making an incense/prayer offering.

NOTE THE FOLLOWING QUOTES RELATING TO THE USE OF MARIJUANA AS INCENSE:

"It is said that the Assyrians used hemp (marijuana) as incense in the seventh or eighth century before Christ and called it 'Qunubu,' a term apparently borrowed from an old East Iranian word 'Konabe,' the same as the Scythian name 'cannabis.'" (Plants of the Gods—Origin of Hallucinogenic Use by Richard E. Schultes and Albert Hofmann)

"It is recorded that the Chinese Taoist recommended the addition of cannabis to their incense burners in the 1st century as a means of achieving immortality." (*"Marijuana, the First Twelve Thousand Years"* by Ernest Abel, page 5)

"There is a classic Greek term, cannabeizein, which means to smoke cannabis. Cannabeizein frequently took the form of inhaling vapors from an incense burner in which these resins were mixed with other resins, such as myrrh, balsam, frankincense, and perfumes."(Ritual Use of Cannabis Sativa L.)

Herodotus in the fifth century B.C. observed the Scythians throwing hemp on heated stones to create smoke. And, the smoke was inhaled. Although he does not identify them, Herodotus states that when they "have parties and sit around a fire, they throw some of it into the flames. As it burns, it smokes like incense, and the smell of it makes them drunk, just as wine does us. As more fruit is thrown on, they get more and more intoxicated until finally they jump up and start dancing and singing." (Herodotus, Histories 1 .202.)

Tracing the history of hemp in terms of cultural contacts, the Old Testament must not be overlooked since it provides one of the oldest and most important written source materials. In the original Hebrew text of the Old Testament there are references to hemp, both as incense, which was an integral part of religious celebrations, and as an intoxicant (Benet 1936). Cannabis as an incense was also used in the temples of Assyria and Babylon "because its aroma was pleasing to the Gods."(Meissner 1925 (11184).

EVIDENCE INDICATING THE SEMITIC ORIGIN OF CANNABIS

In 1903, British Physician and Biblical scholar Dr. C. Creighton released a book entitled "Evidence of the Hashish Vice in the Old Testament." In this volume, Dr. Creighton put forth a theory that cannabis was the grass eaten by Nebuchadnezzar; it was responsible for the strength of Samson and Jonathan, and the Prophet Ezekiel's vision (*"I will raise up for them a plant of renown, and they shall be no more consumed with hunger in the land, neither bear the shame of the heathen any more"* — Ezekiel 34:29).

Like the ancient Greeks, the Old Testament Israelites were surrounded by marijuana-using peoples. Dr. C. Creighton concluded that several references to marijuana can be found in the Old Testament. Examples are: the "honeycomb" referred to in the Song of Solomon, 5: 1, and the "honeywood" in 1 Samuel 14: 25-45. (Others have suggested that the "calamus" in the Song of Solomon was in fact cannabis).

(Mention of Creighton's book can be found in "Licit and Illicit Drugs," by the Editors of Consumer Reports and "Marijuana Reconsidered" by Lester Grinspoon)

Cannabis use in the Old Testament was again looked at in 1936, by Sula Benet, who stated that the original Hebrew text contains references to hemp as both an intoxicant and incense. Similar results were found in 1946 by Sara Benetowa, of the Institute of Anthropological Science in Warsaw, referring to the Old Testament Hebrew word "kanehbosm" (fragrant reed).

This word appeared in Exodus 30:23, Isaiah 43:24, Jeremiah 6:20, Ezekiel 27: 19, Song of Solomon 4:14, and has been erroneously translated as calamus and sweet calamus in modern Bibles (from "Cannabis and Culture," Vera Rubin [editor], and "The Book of Grass," edited by Andrews and Vinkenoog).

Benetowa's research includes Exodus, the story of Moses, as having references to *kanehbosm* (hemp). I am sure most readers are aware that "The Angel (angel comes from the Greek word *'angelo'* meaning messenger) of the Lord appeared to Moses in flames of fire from within a bush". Exodus 3:2.

It is interesting to note that the use of incense in the Bible was instituted by Moses. (It is also interesting to note that early East Indian legends maintained that the angel of mankind lives in the leaves of the hemp plant, and the Zend-Avesta [Zoroastrian Holy Books] refers to the soma, a possible hemp beverage, as both a plant and an angel).

The name cannabis is generally thought to be of Scythian origin. Sula Benet, in *Cannabis and Culture*, argues that it has a much earlier origin in Semitic languages like Hebrew, occurring several times in the Old Testament. He states that in Exodus 30:23 God commands Moses to make a holy anointing oil of myrrh, sweet cinnamon, kanehbosm, and kassia.

He continues that the word "Kanehbosm" is also rendered in traditional Hebrew as "kannabus" or "kannabus"; the root "kan" in this construction means "reed" or "hemp," while "bosm" means "aromatic."

Benet also resumes that in the earliest Greek translations of the Old Testament "kan" was translated as "sweet calamus" (Exodus 30:23), "Sweet cane" (Isaiah 43:24; Jeremiah 6:20) and "calamus" (Ezekiel 27: 19; Song of Solomon 4:14). He argues from the linguistic evidence that cannabis was known in Old Testament times, at least for its aromatic properties; hence, the word had passed from the Semitic language to the Scythians, i.e. the Ashkenaz of the Old Testament.

Sara Benetowa is quoted in the Book of Grass as saying:

"The astonishing resemblance between the Semitic "kanbos" and the Scythian "cannabis" leads me to suppose that the Scythian word was of Semitic origin, These etymological discussions run parallel to arguments drawn from history. The Iranian Scythians were probably related to the Medes, who were neighbors of the Semites and could easily have assimilated the word for hemp. The Semites could also have spread the word during their migrations through Asia Minor. Taking into account the matriarchal element of Semitic culture, one is led to believe that Asia Minor was the original point of expansion for both the society based on the matriarchal circle and the mass use of hashish."

The ancient Israelites were a Semitic people. Abraham, the father of the Israelite nation, came from Ur, a city of Babylonia located in Mesopotamia (Asia Minor). The Israelites migrated throughout Asia Minor and could have been instrumental in spreading the religious use of marijuana.

CHAPTER 14
"THE ISRAELITE USE OF INCENSE"

The use of incense in the Bible was instituted by Moses. Moses discovered the Angel of the Lord in flames of fire from within a bush. (Exodus 3:2)

Incense was assigned miraculous powers by the Israelites. It was burned in golden bowls or cauldrons placed on or beside the altar. It was also burned in hand-held censers. In the Blessing of Moses, a poem belonging to the Northern Kingdom of Israel, and written about 760 B.C., the sacrificial smoke is offered to the God of Israel:

"Let them teach Jacob thy judgments, and Israel thy law; Let them offer sacrificial smoke to thy nostrils, and whole burnt sacrifice upon thine altar."

Throughout the Bible, the ancient patriarchs were brought into communion with God through smoking incense. At Mt. Sinai God talked to Moses out of a bush that burned with fire (Exodus 3:12). In addition, after Moses brought the Israelite people out of Egypt he returned to Mt. Sinai, at which time God made a covenant with Moses in which the Ten Commandments were revealed. Exodus 19:8 describes the conditions at the time of this covenant.

"And Mount Sinai was altogether on smoke, because the Lord descended upon it in fire: and the smoke thereof ascended as smoke of a furnace, and the whole mount quaked greatly."

The mysterious smoke mentioned in the covenant on Mt. Sinai is also referred to as a cloud:

Exodus 24:15-16 —*"[15]Moses went up into the mount, and a cloud covered the mount. [16] And the glory of the Lord abode upon Mount Sinai, and the cloud covered it six days: and the seventh he called unto Moses out of the midst of the cloud."*

The scriptures make it abundantly clear that the cloud and the smoke are related to the burning of incense. Exodus 40: 26 describes Moses burning incense – a cloud covering the tent of the congregation and the glory of the Lord filling the tabernacle.

Leviticus 16:2-13 describes how God appeared in a cloud; this cloud is referred to as the cloud of incense. Numbers 16: 17-19 demonstrates that every man of the congregation had a censer filled with burning incense and the glory of the Lord appeared unto the entire congregation.

Isaiah shows that Ezekiel saw God in a smoke-filled inner court. Numbers 11:25 illustrates that God was revealed to Moses and the seventy elders in a cloud; that the spirit rested upon them and they prophesied and ceased not.

The Book of Grass, by Andrew and Vinkenoog, includes a section on Ancient Scythia and Iran by Mircea Eliade, one of the foremost experts on the history of religions. On pages 11 and 12 is the following:

> *"On one document appears to indicate the existence of a Getic shamanism: It is Strabo's account of the Myssian KAPNOBATAI, a name that has been translated, by analogy with Aristophanes' AEROBATES as 'those who walk in clouds'; but should be translated as 'those who walk in smoke!' Presumably the smoke is hemp smoke, a rudimentary means of ecstasy known to both the Thracians and the Scythians…"*

This passage should be carefully noted. Biblical passages make it abundantly clear that the ancient Israelites also walked in clouds and in smoke. In fact, it was in the clouds of smoke that God was revealed to the ancient Israelites. The words "smoke" and "smoking" appear fifty times in the King James Version of the Bible, and two separate times the Bible says of the Lord, "There went up a smoke out of his nostrils." II Samuel 22:9, Psalms 18:8.

In Isaiah 6: 6 – "Seraphim" means literally "Smoke Drinker."

Sara Benetowa mentioned that in the Old Testament Isaiah refers to hemp as coal or incense, which the hashish form or cannabis burns like, and it is in that chapter we find the following; the setting is a temple filled with smoke:

Isaiah 6:4 *"And the posts of the door moved at the voice of him that cried, and the house was filled with smoke."*

6:5 *"Then said I, Woe is me, for I am undone; because I am a man of unclean lips, and I dwell in the midst of a people of unclean lips; for mine eyes have seen the King, the Lord of hosts."*

6:6 *"Then flew one of the seraphims unto me, having a live coal in his hand, which he had taken with the tongs from of the altar,"*

6:7 *"And he laid it upon my mouth and said, Lo, this hath touched thy lips: and thine iniquity is taken away, and thy sin purged."*

Those of us who are familiar with hashish know that it burns in a similar way to both incense and coal. We have noted the use of marijuana in India, as well as China and Japan, to deter evil and cleanse its user from sin. There are numerous other places in the Bible which mention the burning of incense, the mysterious cloud, and smoke. This common thread is found throughout the Bible, including the New Testament.

St. Matthew 24: 30 *"And then shall appear the sign of the Son of Man in heaven: and then shall all the tribes of the earth mourn, and they shall see the Son of Man coming in the clouds of heaven, with power and great glory."*

Revelations 1:7 *"Behold, he cometh with clouds; and every eye shall See him, and they also which pierced him: and all kindreds of the earth shall wail because of him. Even so, Amen."*

Revelations 8:3 *"And another angel came and stood at the altar, having a golden censer: and there was given unto him much incense, that he should offer it with the prayers of all saints upon the golden altar which was before the throne."*

Revelation 8:4 *"And the smoke of the incense, which came with the prayers of the saints, ascended up before God out of the angel's hand."*

Revelations 15:8 *"And the temple was filled with smoke from the glory of God, and from His power."*

CHAPTER 15
"THE SYMBOLISM OF FIRE IN THE ANCIENT WORLD"

The word "fire" is mentioned several hundred times in the King James Version of the Bible. The sacrifice of the Lord is made by fire (Exodus 29:18, 25; Leviticus 2: 10-11; I Samuel 2: 28; II Chronicles 2:4; Isaiah 24: 15; Matthew 3:11; Luke 1:9; Revelations 8:4-5)

Abraham, the father of the Israelite nation, came from Ur, which was a city in South Babylonia. For the Babylonians, fire was essential to sacrifice, and all oblations were conveyed to the gods by the fire god Girru-Nusku, whose presence as an intermediary between the gods and man was indispensable. Girru-Nusku, as the messenger of the gods, bore the essence of the offerings upward to them in the smoke of the sacrificial fire.

At Babylon: "The glorious gods smell the incense, noble food of heaven; pure wine, which no hand has touched do they enjoy." (L. Jeremias, in Encyclopaedia Biblica, i.v. 4119, quoting Rawlinson, Cuneif. Inscrip. IV, 19 159) – Note the relationship of incense to noble food of heaven and pure wine.

Like their Babylonian neighbors to the west, the most important of the ancient Indian gods was Agni, the god of fire, who like the Babylonian god (Girru-Nusku) acted as a messenger between men and the gods. The fire (Agni) upon the altar was regarded as a messenger – their invoker.

"For thou, O sage, goest wisely between these two creations like a friendly messenger between two hamlets."

CHAPTER 16
"MYSTICISM"

Mysticism is the theory or belief that man can intuitively know God or religious truth through the inward perception of the mind, a more immediate and direct method than that of ordinary understanding or sense perception; any seeking to solve the mysteries of existence by internal illumination or special revelation.

According to the Encyclopedia Britannica, the section on "Mysticism":

> "The Vedas (Hindu sacred writings) are hymns to the mystic fire and the inner sense of sacrifice, burning forever on the 'altar Mind.' Hence the abundance of solar and fire images: birds of fire, the fire of the sun and the isles of fire. The symbol system of the world's religions and mysticisms are profound illuminations of the human-divine mystery. 'Be it the cave of the heart or the lotus of the heart, the dwelling place of that which is the Essence of the Universe, the third eye, or the eye of wisdom—the symbols all refer back to wisdom entering the aspiring soul on its way toward progressive self-understanding. "I saw the Lord with the Eye of the Heart.' I said, 'Who art thou?' and he answered, 'Thou.'"

Mystics from India have said:

> "That in the ecstasy of bhang (marijuana), the spark of the Eternal in man turns into light the murkiness of matter or illusion and the self is lost in the central soul fire. Raising man out of himself and above mean individual worries, bhang makes him one with the divine force of nature and the mystery 'I am he' grew plain." (Taken from the Indian Hemp Drugs Commission Report which was written at the turn of the twentieth century).

The concept of spiritual or inner light was found throughout the ancient world. Light is a very obvious metaphor for godhead; therefore, one would expect it to appear in the symbology of many cultures. As we shall see, spiritual light was directly related to the burning of incense. According to Lucie Lamy in "Egyptian Mysteries", page 24:

"The Pharaonic word for light was akh. This word, often translated as 'transfigured', designated transcendental light as well as all aspects of physical light; and in the funerary text it denotes the State of ultimate sublimation...

"The word akh, first of all, is written with a glyph showing a crested ibis: ibis comata. This bird—the name of which was also akh— lived in the southern part of the Arabian side of the Red Sea (near Al Qunfudhah) and migrated to Abyssinia (Ethiopia) during the winter. Both these places are near the regions from which sacred incense came, and were called the 'Divine Land'. The bird's crest, together with its dark green plumage, shot with glittering metallic specks, justifies the meanings 'to shine', 'to be resplendent', 'to irradiate'; of the root akh in the hieroglyphic writing...

"Akh indeed expresses all notions of light, both literally and figuratively, from the Light which comes forth from darkness to the transcendental light of transfiguration. It is also used to designate the 'third eye', the Uraeus, related in old tradition to the pineal body and to the spirit."

Note the following concerning the transfiguration of Christ:

St. Matthew 17: 1-5 *"And after six days Jesus taketh peter, James, and John his brother, and bringeth them up into a high mountain apart.²And was transfigured before them: and his face did shine as the sun, and his raiment was white as light. ³ And, behold there appeared unto them Moses and Eli'jah talking with him. ⁴ Then answered peter, and said unto Jesus, Lord, it is good for us to be here: if thou wilt, let us make here three tabernacles; one for thee, one for Moses, and one for Eli'jah. ⁵When he yet spake, behold a bright cloud overshadowed them: and behold, a voice out of the cloud, which said, This is my beloved Son, in whom I am well pleased; hear ye him."*

The Bible Dictionary by John McKenzie, page 898, says concerning the transfiguration, that the cloud and the formula of the utterance of the father are derived from the baptism of Jesus. He further states that the change described in the appearance of Jesus suggests the change which is implied in the resurrection narratives.

Some of the synonyms of transfiguration are transformation, metamorphosis, transubstantiation, and avatar. These terms imply the change that accompanies resurrection or deification.

Across the world, legends of godlike men who managed to rise in a state of perfection, go back to an era before human beings had cast away from the divine source. Hence, the gods were beings which once were men, and the actual race of men will in time become gods. Christ revealed this to the people of his day when he told them to whom the word of God came, "Ye are gods." (St. John 10:34)

St. Matthew 17:2 says that during the transfiguration of Christ, his face did shine as the sun. The face of Moses also shone when he returned from the cloud on Mt. Sinai (Exodus 30:34). The shining countenances are the result of their resurrections, of their being spiritually illuminated in the cloud of smoking incense.

Note the following taken from Eliades – "A History of Religious Ideas, Vol. 1 from the Stone Age to the Eleusinian Mysteries":

"The state of maga is obtained primarily by the Haoma sacrifice, the sacrifice of the "drink of immortality", which the priest imbibes during the ceremony. Now haoma is rich in xvarenah, the sacred fluid, at once igneous, luminous, vivifying, and spermatic. Ahura Mazda is preeminently the possessor of xvarenah, but this divine "flame" also springs from the forehead of Mithra (Yast 10. 127) and, like a solar light, emanates from the heads of sovereigns. However, every human being possesses his xvarenah, and on the day of transfiguration, i.e., of the final Renovation, "the great light seeming to come from the body will burn continually on this earth." By ritually absorbing haoma the sacrifice surpasses his human condition, comes close to Ahura Mazda (name of Zoroastrian God), and anticipates in concerto the universal renovation."

Eliade postulates that the haoma sacrifice was a marijuana drink like the bhang of India. And as mentioned earlier, the devotee who partook of Bhang, also partook of Shiva – awakening his eye of Shiva.

Famed author, mystic, and an 18th-century member of "Le

Club des Haschischins," Charles Baudelaire, said that the use of hashish gave one "the strange power of smoking yourself..." It's no wonder that the early Catholic Church placed cannabis ingestion with cannibalism; perhaps there is even a correlation between the two words.

George Gurdjieff, the famed Russian mystic, spent years in the monasteries of the Sufis in the Hindu-Kush. The Sufis are well-known for their use of hashish, which was introduced by Haydar, the founder of the herb.

Charles T. Tart's book on the teachings of Gurdjieff, draws the similarities between an unknown drug Gurdjieff had used on some subjects and marijuana:

"If you could just suddenly be your essence, it would be a great relief for a while, but eventually quite tiring. Essence stopped growing in early childhood, and it's difficult to live an adult life as a child. Gurdjieff reportedly demonstrated this by temporarily returning a person to essence, using a combination of unknown drugs and hypnosis. Recall the phenomenon of hypnotic age regression discussed in Chapter 9. In my study of marijuana intoxication, I found one of the most common effects to be that of feeling more childlike and open, an obvious component of the drug's appeal. For permanent results though, we need to rediscover essence and then nourish it, love and cherish it, as a more enlightened parent would have done. Since we live in false personality, false personality has to use its best resources to do this.

"Gradually, essence can grow and begin to use the resources, knowledge, and power now automatically used by false personality. Instead of being the usual, say, 2 percent essence and 98 percent false personality, you can get a gradual shift toward more and more essence, more and more vitality and essential joy in life, and less and less false personality. This needs to be accompanied by the development of the higher kind of consciousness we are calling awakening."

It is interesting to note that Christ said: unless you can become like a child, you cannot enter the Kingdom of Heaven. He also stated that the Kingdom of Heaven is within. This age old belief, common in so many of the world's religions, is that the Indian hemp is capable of awakening the "Holy Spirit" that is within us all.

By "Holy Spirit," we mean, the breath or spark of God that lies in the heart of every man, sometimes referred to as the "Higher Self"; the "Eye of Shiva" of the Hindu faith (Siva or Shiva, was also known as the "Lord of Bhang"); the "I Am" of the hashish eating Sufis; the "xvarenah" (khvarenah) of the Magi, who were later known as Zoroastrians, a name derived from that faith's most noble prophet Zoroaster, also known as Zarathustra Spitma, and the "I n I" of the Rastafarian faith, or the "One Mind" of the early Gnostics.

CHAPTER 17
"MARIJUANA AS THE CHRISTIAN SACRAMENT"

The little most people know about the life of Jesus Christ comes from the Bible's New Testament, and this was not compiled into its present form until about three hundred years after Christ's death; this happened when Constantine, the Emperor of Rome, made a politically motivated conversion to Christianity. He formed the Roman Catholic Church and wiped out conflicting sects like the Gnostics and Essenes.

According to Jack Herer in *The Emperor No Clothes or Everything You Wanted to Know About Marijuana But Were Not Taught in School*, "The Essenes, a kabalistic priest/prophet/healer sect of Judaism dating back to the era of the Dead Sea Scrolls, used hemp, as did the Therapeutae of Egypt, from where we get the term 'therapeutic.' "

The Therapeutae of Egypt were Jewish ascetics that dwelt near Alexandria and described by Philo (1st century B.C.) as devoted to contemplation and meditation. Alexandria is where St. Mark is traditionally held to have established the Coptic Church in 45 A.D.

The Egyptian Coptic Church has been neglected by Western scholars despite its historical significance. The result is that the Coptic Church has very little (documented) history. This has been due to the various biases of the Catholic Church which claimed Christianity for its own self-interest. However, it's assumed that the Coptic religious services have their roots in the earliest layers of Christian ritual in ancient origin, going back to the time of the first Christian communities of Egypt, and even before.

Tradition states that "Coptic" was derived from "Kuftaim," son of Mizraim, a grandchild of Noah who first settled in the Nile valley, in the neighborhood of Thebes, the ancient capital of Egypt. At one time Thebes was the greatest city in the world, and history records that by 2200 B.C. the whole of Egypt was united under a Theban prince. The splendor of Thebes was known to Homer, who called it "the city with a hundred gates." (Richard Schultes states that in ancient Thebes marijuana was made into a drink).

According to E.A. Wallis Budge in *The Divine Origin of the Craft of a Herbalist*, page 79, "The Copts (that is to say the Egyptians who accepted the teachings of St. Mark in the first century of our era and embraced Christianity) seem to have eschewed medical science as taught by the physicians of the famous School of Medicine of Alexandria, and to have been content with the methods of healing employed by their ancestors."

The Essenes were an ascetic sect closely related to the Therapeutae that had established a monastic order in the desert outside of Palestine, and were known as spiritual healers. It has been suggested that both John the Baptist and Jesus may have been of the Essene sect as they were both heavily dependent on Essene teachings. The scripture makes no mention of the life of Jesus from the age of 13 to 30. Certain theologians speculate that Jesus was being initiated by the Essenes, the last fraternity to keep alive the ancient traditions of the prophets. Scripture indicates that Christ spent time in Egypt. (See also: The Aquarian Gospel of Jesus, the Christ.)

Every prophet, however great, must be initiated. His higher self must be awakened and made conscious so that his mission can be fulfilled. Amongst the Essenes, rituals preceded most liturgical rites, the most important one of which was participation in a sacred meal—an anticipation of the Messianic banquet.

Throughout the ancient world, sacrifice was a sacramental communal meal involving the idea of the god as a participant in the meal or identical with the food consumed. The communion sacrifice was one in which the deity indwells the oblation so that the worshippers actually consume the divine. The original motive of sacrifice was an effort toward communion among the members of a group, on one hand, and between them and their god, on the other. At its best, sacrifice was a "sacrament" and in one form or another, life itself.

Philo, the famous ancient Egyptian historian, noted that Jesus was a member of the brotherhood of Egyptian seers known as the Essene.

Zoroastrian priestly castes in ancient Media and Persia were also referred to as the Magi; the Magi were the pioneers of magnetism, science, and astrology. Thus, they predicted the coming of Christ; the "Three Magi followed the Star to Bethlehem. They brought incense, myrrh, and gold as gifts." Is it too much to put forth that these same Magi who showed such a keen interest in the baby Jesus, would later want to be part of his spiritual development?

If Christ was born with total consciousness, there would have been accounts of miracles performed by the boy Jesus. It is far more likely that the skills referred to as miracles were developed later in Jesus' life (when he was mature enough to handle such powers), under the skill and tutelage of the most advanced scientists and magicians of that time: the ancient Magi. It is most likely through them, that Christ was initiated into the deep secret of the true Eucharist, the Soma, an Indian Hemp beverage referred to as the "New Wine" in Christian literature.

The Eucharist is one of the most simple and complete magic ceremonies. When you take something, and with prayer, transmute it into the divine, then ingest it, over a period of time matter is replaced by *spirit*. Day by day, that person will become, in truth, the Temple of the Holy Spirit.

This ceremony is intensified with hemp because cannabis is a hypnotic drug, this is why, when marijuana was used as a medicine in America in the 1900s, there was very little reference to people becoming intoxicated by it. They were hypnotized into getting the effects that they expected from it. It is for this same reason that first-time users often feel little or no effect from smoking hemp: they are not sure what effects to look for.

The central focus of the early Christian church was the Eucharist or the "body and blood" of the Lord. This was interpreted as a fellowship meal with the resurrected Christ. In meeting the Resurrected One in the Eucharist meal, the Christian community had the expectation of the kingdom of God and salvation.

In 1949, a Gnostic library was found on the upper Nile River in Egypt. It is the only remaining library of Gnostic literature and it has revolutionized the understanding of Christianity. These works are known as "The Nag Hammadi Codices." The Bible is largely based upon Gnosticism. When Jesus told his disciples that he spoke in parables, that only those who were supposed to understand could do so, *he* was practicing Gnosticism at its most basic.

The Nag Hammadi Library in English:

> "As we discussed the robbers on the road, whom we evaded, behold Lithargoel, having changed, came out to us. He had the appearance of a physician, since an

unguent box was under his arm, and a young disciple was following him, carrying a pouch full of medicine. We did not recognize him.

"Lithargoel answered, 'I want to ask you who gave the name Peter to you?' He said to him, 'It was Jesus Christ, the son of the living God. He gave this name to me.' He answered and said, 'It is I! Recognize me, Peter.' He loosened the garment, which clothed him - the one into which he had changed himself because of us - revealing to us in truth that it was he.

"We prostrated ourselves on the ground and worshipped him. We comprised eleven disciples. He stretched forth his hand and caused us to stand. We spoke with him humbly. Our heads were bowed down in unworthiness as we said, 'What you wish we will do. But give us power to do what you wish at all times.'

"He gave them the unguent box and the pouch that was in the hand of the young disciple. He commanded them like this, saying, 'Go into the city from which you came, which is called Habitation. Continue in endurance as you teach all those who have believed in my name, because I have endured in hardships of the faith. I will give you your reward. To the poor of that city give what they need in order to live until I give them what is better, which I told you that I will give you for nothing.

"Peter answered and said to him, 'Lord, you have taught us to forsake the world and everything in it. We have renounced them for your sake. What we are concerned about now is the food for a single day. Where will we be able to find the needs that you ask us to provide for the poor?'

"The Lord answered and said, 'O Peter, it was necessary that you understand the parable that I told you! Do you not understand that my name, which you teach, surpasses all riches, and the wisdom of God surpasses gold, and silver and precious stones?'

"He gave them the pouch of medicine and said, 'Heal all the sick of the city who believe in my name...

"He answered them, 'Rightly have you spoken, John,

for I know that the physicians of this world heal what belongs to the world. The physicians of souls, however, heal the heart. Heal the bodies first; therefore, so that through the powers of healing for their bodies, without medicine of the world, they may believe in you, that you have power to heal the illnesses of the heart also.' "

Christ communicated life to his disciples through the Eucharist or Christian sacrament. Christ said in describing the sacrament, "Take, eat, this is my body; this is my blood. Do this as often as you will in remembrance of me." (1 Corinthians 11:24-25)

CHAPTER 18
"BAPTISM"

Baptism is defined as the Christian sacrament used in purification and the spiritual rebirth of the individual. 1 Corinthians 10:1-4 makes it clear that the smoking cloud of incense was directly related to baptism.

1 Corinthians 10: 1-4 "*[1]Moreover, brethren, I would not that ye should be ignorant, how that our fathers were under the cloud, and all passed through the sea; [2] And were all baptized unto Moses in the Cloud and in the sea,[3]And did all eat the same spiritual meat; [4]And did all drink the same spiritual drink: for they drank of that Spiritual Rock that followed them: and that Rock was Christ."*

Here the mysterious cloud is associated with spiritual meat.

In the Biblical story of Creation, God said, "Behold, I have given you every bearing seed, and to you it will be for meat." (Genesis 1:29) Marijuana is technically a herb, and as we have, was considered a spiritual meat in the ancient world.

From 1 Corinthians 10: 1-4, we see that the spiritual cloud resulting from the burning of incense was instrumental in the baptism of the Israelites. This baptism is also compared to the "eating and drinking" of the spirit of Christ.

Spirit is defined as the active essence of the Deity serving as an invisible and life-giving or inspiring power in motion. Spirit comes from spiritus- breathing; and the biological meaning of inspiration is to breathe or inhale. (The Living Webster Encyclopedic Dictionary of the English language, 1977)

The scripture makes it abundantly clear that the sacrificial cloud of smoke contained the Spirit of God (Christ) and was instrumental in inspiring, sanctifying, and purifying the patriarchs.

In Numbers 11: 25-26 the cloud results in the *spirit* resting upon Moses and the seventy elders. This passage indicates that they prophesied ecstatically. "Prophesy" is defined as follows: to utter or announce by or as if by divine inspiration; to speak for God or a deity, to give instruction in religious matters.

Throughout the Holy Bible, prophets of God spake as they

were moved by the Holy Spirit. The smoking, burning cloud of incense contained the *spirit* and was instrumental in bringing about the spiritual revelations of the prophets. The virtues of marijuana include speech-giving and inspiration of mental powers.

It is recorded in ancient China, that marijuana was used by the Taoist priest to set forward time, in order to reveal future events. Anyone who is familiar with the Bible knows that it is full of prophecies revealing forthcoming events.

"Psycho-active" is defined as affecting the mind or behavior. When we, of the Ethiopian Zion Coptic Church, think of mind or behavior, we think of that inward essence or element that makes up the individual. This is the person's spirit. We are all spiritual beings. It is just as important to keep the spiritual part of a person healthy, as it is to keep the physical body healthy, and in fact, they are related. Hence, marijuana and its purification and protection from evil influences.

Most people are under the impression that Christ baptized with water; as you can see from the following account of John the Baptist, this isn't so. John the Baptist, baptized with water and Christ baptized with fire.

St. Matthew 3:11 *"I indeed baptize you with water unto repentance: but he that cometh after me is mightier than I, whose shoes I am not worthy to bear; he shall baptize you with the Holy Spirit and with fire."*

It is only logical that this baptism with the Holy Spirit and with fire is related to the baptism of Christ, in the burning, smoking cloud of incense, and to the baptism of the patriarchs in which the patriarchs did all eat of the same spiritual meat (incense).

In the section dealing with the "Holy Spirit," the Encyclopedia Britannica states that Christian writers have seen in various references to the Spirit of Yahweh in the Old Testament an anticipation of the doctrine of the Holy Spirit. It also says: the Holy Spirit is viewed as the main agent of man's restoration to his original, natural state through communion in Christ's body; thus, as the principle of life in the Christian community.

The patriarchs were recipients of a revelation coming directly from the *spirit* (incense), and this was expressed in the heightening and enlargement of their consciousness. It is clear from the scripture that this spiritual dimension was also evident in the life of

Jesus, in whom the experiences of the Hebrew prophets were renewed. Through the Eucharist, Christ passed this spiritual dimension on to his apostles. One of the apostles even makes mention in Philippians 4:18 of "a sweet-smelling sacrifice that is well pleasing to God."

Christ compares his baptism to the drinking of a cup.

> St. Mark 10:38 *"But Jesus said unto them, 'Ye know not what ye ask: can ye drink of the cup that I drink of? and be baptized with the baptism that I am baptized with?'"*

This cup is referred to as the cup of salvation in...

> Psalms 116:12: *"What shall I render unto the Lord for all his benefits toward me? I will take the cup of salvation and call upon the name of the Lord."*

There are three things that spread the Christ-life to us: Baptism, Belief, and that mysterious action which different Christians call by various names – *Holy Communion, the Mass*, and *the Lord's Supper*. It is called the Cup of Blessing in connection with the Eucharist.

> 1 Corinthians 10: 16-17"[16]*The cup of blessing which we bless, is it not the communion of the blood and the body of Christ?* [17] *For we being many are one bread, and one body; for we are all partakers of that one bread."*

Here we see a connection between the cup of blessing and the communion of the blood of Christ. Blood is the life-giving substance of the living being. Christ communicated life to his disciples through the Eucharist or Christian sacrament.

In 1 Corinthians 10:16-17 we note the mention of bread in the communion of the body of Christ and that we are all "partakers of one bread." This is the spiritual bread or food used by Christ and his disciples. A synonym for the Eucharist or Body and Blood of the Lord is the "bread of Life." It is interesting to note that the finest marijuana in Jamaica today, is called "Lamb's Bread."

> 1 Corinthians 12: 13 *"For by one Spirit are we all baptized into one body, whether we be Jews or Gentiles, whether we be bond or free; and have been all made to drink into one Spirit."*

1 Corinthians 11:25-26 *"After the same manner also he took the cup, when he had supped, saying, "This cup is the new testament in my blood: this do ye, as oft as ye drink it, in remembrance of me.* ^{26} *For as often as ye eat this bread, and drink this cup, do shew the Lord's death till he come."*

If these passages are compared to 1 Corinthians 10: 1-4, it is plain that the "eating of one bread" is the same as the patriarchs "eating the same spiritual meat" and the "drinking of one Spirit" (the cup); it's the same as the patriarchs "drinking of the Spiritual Rock that followed them: and that rock was Christ."

By making this comparison, we see that the terminology of the Eucharist is directly related to the smoking cloud of incense used in the baptism of Christ and the patriarchs.

It is interesting to note that smoking was referred to as "eating" or "drinking" by the early American Indians. Peter T. Furst in *Hallucinogens and Culture* states the following:

> *"Considering its enormous geographic spread in the Americas at the time of European discovery, as well as the probable age of stone tobacco pipes in California, the inhaling (often called "drinking" or "eating") of tobacco smoke by the Shaman, as a corollary to therapeutic fumigation and the feeding of the gods with smoke, must also be of considerable antiquity."*

In *Licit and Illicit Drugs*, page 209, the following is quoted:

> *"Columbus and other early explorers who followed him were amazed to meet Indians who carried rolls of dried leaves that they set afire – and who then 'drank the smoke' that emerged from the rolls. Other Indians carried pipes in which they burned the same leaves, and from which they similarly 'drank the smoke.'"*

The Encyclopedia Britannica states in the section on "Sacrifice" that the interpretation of sacrifice and particularly of the Eucharist, as a sacrifice, has varied greatly within the different Christian traditions, because the sacrificial terminology in which the Eucharist was originally described became foreign to Christian thinkers.

We of the Ethiopian Zion Coptic Church declare: the true understanding of the Eucharist has been passed down from generation to generation, so that we are able to give an accurate interpretation of the sacrificial terminology used to describe the Eucharist. We have shown, using history and Biblical passages, that his terminology is directly related to burning, smoking incense. We have shown that the "eating" or "drinking" contained in the terminology concerning the Eucharist is associated with the inhalation of smoke. We have shown that marijuana was used as incense and it was the number-one spiritual plant of the ancient world.

We of the Ethiopian Zion Coptic Church declare: the cup that Christ baptized his disciples with, in the baptism of the Holy Spirit and fire, was in fact, a pipe or "chillum" in which marijuana was smoked. This is a bottomless cup and soon as it is emptied – it is filled again and passed in a circle.

Like the pipe of the ancient North American Indians, this Cup was a portable altar.

Christ was the Father of the doctrine of the Eucharist, which is the communion that Jesus gave his brethren. Jesus taught of the Communion as his body and blood. Jesus was not speaking of the physical body and blood. He was speaking of his spiritual body and spiritual blood that was the communion of his Holy church. The supper Jesus celebrated with his disciples *"on the night that he was betrayed"* (1 Corinthians 11:23) inaugurated the heavenly meal that was to be continued.

1 Corinthians 11: 23-29 *"For I have received of the Lord that which also I delivered unto you, that the Lord Jesus the same night in which he was betrayed took bread:* [24] *And when he had given thanks, he broke it and said 'Take, eat, this is my body, which is broken for you; this do in remembrance of me'.* [25] *After the same manner also he took the cup, which he had supped, saying, 'This cup is the new testament in my blood; this do ye, as oft as ye drink it, in remembrance of me.* [26]*For as often as ye eat this bread, and drink of this cup, ye do shew the Lord's death till he come.* [27] *Wherefore whosoever shall eat of this bread, and drink of this cup of the Lord unworthily, shall be guilty of the body and blood of the Lord.*[28] *But let a man examine himself, and let him eat of the bread, and drink of that cup.* [29]*For he that eateth and drinketh unworthily, eateth and drinketh damnation to himself, not discerning the Lords body.'"*

Christ said, "Do this in remembrance of me." Here the original unity of man with God is restored. In general, the reception of the Holy Spirit is connected with the actual realization: the inward experience of God.

Marijuana has been referred to as a mild euphoric (the producer of a feeling of well-being) that produces a profound religious experience of a mystical and transcendental nature. This religious experience is said to be brought about by the stirring of deeply buried, unconscious sensitivities, so that one experiences ultimate reality of the divine, and confirms the feeling of the worshipper that he has been in the presence of God and has assimilated some of His powers.

To be lifted above sense, to behold the beatific vision and become "incorporated" in God, is the end sought in ecstasy. The priest or mystic, in enthusiasm or ecstasy, enjoys the beatific by entering into communion with God and by undergoing deification. The experience of ecstasy states Mircea Eliade - one of the foremost authorities on religion - is a timeless primary phenomenon. Psychological experience of rapture, he continues, are fundamental to the human condition; hence, known to the whole of archaic humanity. (Some of the synonyms of rapture are bliss, beatitude, transport, exaltation)

The Hashish club listed, on its membership, literary giants such as Alexandre Dumas, Coleridge, Gautier, De Quincy, Balzac, Baudelaire and Victor Hugo.

Baudelaire, a member of the Club Des Hashischins (Hashish Club), founded in Paris around 1835, and writer of Artificial Paradise, states the following about hashish (Hashish is the unadulterated resin from the flowering tops of the female hemp plant):

> "One will find in hashish nothing miraculous, absolutely nothing but an exaggeration of the natural. The brain and organism on which hashish operates will produce only the normal phenomena peculiar to that individual— increased, admittedly, in number and force, but always faithful to the original. A man will never escape from his destined physical and moral temperament: hashish will be a mirror of his impression and private thoughts — a magnifying mirror, it is true, but only a mirror."

He cautions that the user must be in the right frame of mind to take hashish, for just as it exaggerates the natural behavior of the individual, so too, does hashish intensify the user's immediate feelings. Baudelaire describes three successive phases a hashish user will pass through. He discloses: the final stage is marked by a feeling of calmness in which time and space have no meaning, and there is a sense that one has transcended matter. In this state, one final Supreme thought breaks into consciousness: "I have become God."

Walter de la Mare said, "*Like Opium, it (hashish) induces an extravagant sense of isolation and he went on to quote the experience of his friend Redwood Anderson, who reported on the effect of taking small doses of the drug. He was able to describe the euphoria, the rush of ideas, and the intense subjective feelings of awareness and heightened significance of all his perceptions; but he was not seduced by this near- ecstasy, rather struggling to resist the weakening of voluntary control and to repudiate these illusions of godlike intuition."*(*The Marijuana Papers* by David Solomon, pg. 70)

Realization of one's union with God is necessary in understanding the true Christian sacrament. The understanding of man's relationship to God and God's relationship to man (God in Man and Man in God) was quite prevalent in the ancient world, particularly among the religions that utilized marijuana as part of their religious practice.

The Hindu sage (Manu), states, "He who, in his own soul perceives the Supreme Soul in all beings and acquires equanimity toward them all, attains the highest bliss." To recognize the oneness of self with God was contained in all the teachings of Gautama Buddha.

In the Liturgy of Mithra (the Persian god of light and truth) the suppliant prays, "abide with me in my soul; leave me not," and "that I may be initiated and that the Holy Spirit may breathe within me."

The communion became as intimate as to pass into identity: "I am thou and thou art I." Athanasius, an Ethiopian Saint, theologian, ecclesiastical statesman, and national leader who was closely tied to the Coptic Church in Egypt said, "Even we may become gods walking in the flesh," and "God became man that man might become God."

Western theology (Catholic and Protestant) teaches that the spirit created matter but remained aloof of it. In Hinduism and other eastern religions, the spirit is the inside, the matter is the outside; the two are inseparable. Eastern theologians have rightly perceived that the God one worships must possess all the aspects of his worshippers' nature as well as his own divine nature. Otherwise, how can he create beings whose nature is entirely foreign to his own? What then, would be the meaning of the Biblical phrase: "God made man in his own image?"

Eckhart von Hochheim O.P., commonly known as Meister Eckhart, German theologian, who taught that there is a ground of the soul which is of a level with the divine, with which and through which we may realize God, was accused of heresy. When he died, he was preparing his defense against charges which were to be laid against him in Avignon. They had been brought with all the authority of Pope John XXII behind them. Among the points in his teachings they condemned, was his argument of a common divinity between man and God. For centuries, inquisitors were busy burning mystics for their adherence to such beliefs.

The fact that modern Christendom has no sense of union with God has led to numerous churches being without the understanding for building a Christian culture and kingdom to replace the confusion of modern politics. This understanding was not lacking in the ancient church and was a major source of enthusiasm for the prophets of old.

In fact, the power of the early church was manifested due to this understanding of the spirit of God dwelling in man, the temple of God. To the ancient prophets it was not a God above, nor a God over yonder, but a God within.

"Be still and know that I am God," (psalms 46) — for the visionaries and mystics of every time and place: this has been the first and greatest of the commandments.

In 1 Corinthians 11: 28 Christ said, "Let a man examine himself, and so let him eat of the bread, and drink of the cup." Probably the most relevant study to date about what might be considered typical marijuana experience concludes that marijuana gives spontaneous insights into self. (Dr. Charles Tart, "On Being

Stoned: A Psychological Study of Marijuana Intoxication," Science and Behavior, 1971).

CHAPTER 19
"THE NEW WINE"

"Give yourself gladness from the true vine of Christ. Satisfy yourself with the true vine in which there is no drunkenness or error. For it (the true wine) marks the end of drinking, since there is usually in it what gives joy to the soul and mind through the spirit of God. But first, nurture your reasoning powers before you drink of it."

~ The Teachings of Silvanus ~

From "The Nag Hammadi" library, the Coptic Gnostic Gospels that were buried around 300 A.D. and found in 1945.

The sacramentality of marijuana is declared by Christ himself and can be understood only when a person partakes of the natural divine herb. The fact is, the communion of Jesus cannot be disputed or destroyed.

Marijuana is the new wine divine, and cannot be compared to the old wine, which is alcohol. Jesus rejected the old wine and glorified "new wine" at the wedding feast of Cana. Cana is a linguistic derivation of the present day cannabis... and so it is. (Some Biblical scholars— have looked upon the miracle of Cana as a sign of the Eucharist— and there is a certain amount of support in early tradition for the view).

Note the references to new wine in the Bible:

Isaiah 65:8 *"Thus saith the lord, As the new wine is found in the cluster, and one saith, Destroy it not; for a blessing is in it; so will I do my servant's sake, that I may not destroy them all."*

Acts 2:13 *"Others mocking said, 'These men are full new wine.'"*

Isaiah 65:8 declares that the new wine is found in the cluster and that a blessing is in it. When one mentions clusters, one thinks of, clusters of grapes. Webster's New Riverside Dictionary, Office Edition; as mentioned earlier on page 13, defines marijuana: 1.

Hemp; 2. The dried flower clusters and leaves of the hemp plant, esp. when taken to induce euphoria.

The Encyclopedia Britannica says the following about hemp: Seed producing flowers from elongate, spikelike clusters growing on the pistillate, or female plants; pollen-producing flowers from many branched clusters, or staminate on male plants. Here, and in Webster's dictionary, marijuana fits the description of new wine, and as history has shown, a blessing is in it.

Baudelaire said the following about the effects of hashish:

> "This marvelous experience often occurs as if it were the effect of superior and invisible power acting on the person from without...This delightful and singular state gives no advanced warning. It is as unexpected as a ghost, an intermittent haunting from which we must draw, if we are wise, the certainty of a better existence. This acuteness of thought, this enthusiasm of the senses and the spirit must have appeared throughout the ages as the first blessing."

In the books of Acts, the apostles were accused of being full of new wine. Acts 2: 13 was the time of Pentecost when the Holy Spirit descended upon the apostles. Numerous outpourings of the *spirit* are mentioned in the Acts of the Apostles in which healing, prophesy, and the expelling of demons are particularly associated with the activity of the *spirit*. Incense (marijuana) was used by the ancients for healing, prophesy, and the expelling of demons as well.

When Christ ascended into heaven in the cloud (Acts 1:9-11) he sent his disciples the Holy Spirit with the gift of tongues like as of fire, and it sat upon each of them; they were filled with the Holy *spirit* and were given the power to speak a language that all men could understand. The fiery tongues expressed the power to prophesy or witness. (Marijuana has been credited with speech giving and inspiration of mental powers).

The first two gifts of the Holy Spirit are traditionally said to be wisdom and understanding, which are seriously the two most needed things by the human race. In Jamaica today, marijuana is referred to as the "weed of wisdom" and is reputed to be the plant that grew on Solomon's grave, a man known for his great wisdom. Marijuana expands consciousness and enhances the capacity for mystical and creative inspiration.

In Acts 2:3 fire speaks figuratively of the Holy Spirit. Fire was also a means in which to transport a saint to heaven.

2 Kings 2:*11* "*And it came to pass, as they still went on, and talked, that, behold, there appeared a chariot of fire, and horses of fire, and parted them both asunder; and Elijah went up by a whirlwind into heaven.*"

Recent writers have speculated that this passage was in reference to flying saucers. That is because they look at this passage physically. This ascension of Elijah, like the ascension of Christ in the cloud into heaven, is the "withdrawal" from the external or physical world, to the inner or spiritual world: to be the inmost reality of all. This can be referred to as ecstasy, rapture, or transport, and is a result of the Holy Spirit.

Ecstasy, rapture, or transport; consequently, agrees in designating a feeling or state of intense, often extreme, mental and emotional exaltation. Rapture is defined as ecstatic joy or delight, joyful ecstasy; some of the synonyms of rapture are bliss, beatitude, transport, and exultation. The true rapture; therefore, is one in which one is spiritually transported to the heavens. Don't expect to float up into the sky.

For other references to the *new wine*, we have to look at sources that were not available for editing by the newly formed Roman Catholic Church. In the Dead Sea Scrolls: "Rule for all the Congregation," we again find references to the "new wine"— "...when they are gathered at the communion table or to drink the new wine, and the communion table laid out, and the new wine mixed for drinking...," obviously a ceremony done in remembrance of the Messianic Banquet.

In the Gnostic Scriptures: "Teachings of Silvanus," the "new wine" is referred to as the "true wine of Christ," as we see in the following excerpt:

> "*Give yourself gladness from the true vine of Christ. Satisfy yourself with the true wine in which there is no drunkenness nor error. For it (the true wine) marks the end of drinking, since there is usually in it what gives joy to the soul and mind through the Spirit of God. But first, nurture your reasoning powers before you drink of it (the true wine).*"

"But first nurture your reasoning powers before you drink of it." This sounds like some healthy advice to give first-time partakers of the herb. Additionally, in "The Teachings of Silvanus" Christ is equated with the *Tree of Life*. "For the Tree of Life is Christ, He is Wisdom; he is also the word, he is the life, the power and the door." We have already made one comparison from Hindu Mythology concerning the *Tree of life*, (the Ganja along the Ganges River – the tree of life along the river of life), and now we will look at another.

In India, the devotee who partakes of bhang, the Indian hemp beverage, partakes of the supreme Hindu deity, Shiva, in a similar manner to the Christian Eucharist, and like Shiva being hemp, Christ is equated with the tree of life. Likewise, Hinduism and Zoroastrianism come from one older root source.

History has shown marijuana as the catalyst used to achieve the spiritual journey into the heavens. One dictionary defines marijuana as the leaves and flowering tops when taken to induce euphoria. Euphoria is defined by the same dictionary as great happiness or bliss. Bliss is defined as the ecstasy of salvation; spiritual joy.

Throughout the ancient world, there is mention of "magical flight," "ascent to heaven" and "mystical journey." All these mythological and folklore traditions have their point of departure in an ideology and technique of ecstasy that imply "journey in spirit."

The pilgrimage from earth to heaven is not a journey to some other place or some other time, but is a journey within. One must realize that "death" through which we must pass before God can be seen, does not lie ahead of us in time. Rather it is now that we have a man of sin within us that must be killed and a new man free from sin that must be born.

This is actualized in baptism and the sacramental life of the church "For as many of you as have been baptized into Christ, have put on Christ" (Galatians 3:27). The effect of baptism is spiritual regeneration or rebirth, whereby one is "christened," involving both unions with Christ and remission of sins. In Titus 3:5, baptism is the "bath of regeneration" accompanying renewal by the spirit. Some of the synonyms of regeneration are beatification, conversion, sanctification, salvation, inspiration, bread of life, Body and Blood of Christ.

Sara Benetowa, of the Institute of Anthropological Sciences in Warsaw, is quoted in the Book of Grass as saying:

> "By comparing the old Slavic word 'Kepati' and the Russian 'Kupati' with the Scythian 'cannabis', Shrader developed and justified Meringer's supposition that there is a link between the Scythian baths and Russian vapor baths.

> "In the entire Orient, even today, to 'go to the bath' means not only to accomplish an act of purification and enjoy a pleasure, but also to fulfill the divine law. Vambery calls 'bath' any club in which the members play checkers, drink coffee, and smoke hashish or tobacco."

St. Matthew's account of the institution of the Eucharist attaches to the Eucharist Cup these words: "Drink of it, all of it, for this is the blood of the covenant, which is poured out for many for the remission of sins" (St. Matthew 26:27). Drinking the sacramental cup; therefore, serves like baptism: (Acts 2:38) where Peter said unto them, "Repent, and be baptized every one of you in the name of Jesus Christ for the remission of sins, and ye shall receive the gift of the Holy Spirit." We of the Ethiopian Zion Coptic Church declare a three-part doctrine of the Holy Herb, the Holy Word, and the Holy Man (Woman).

The present and future benefits to the individual communicant have their importance given to them by Jesus, who said, "He who eats my flesh and drinks my blood has eternal life, and I will raise them up at the last day." (John 6: 54) As such we must see that the divine person who is active in creation, in renewal, and in human rebirth and resurrection, is also active in the Eucharist.

There was a profound change in America when marijuana smoking started on a large scale in the late 1960s. A large number of people resisted the draft, resisted the war...started letting their hair and beards grow...became interested in natural foods...the ecology and the environment.

What we really saw was the awakening of our generation; the beginning of Christian mentality through marijuana smoking. The earmarks of this mentality are: I don't want to go to war; I really don't want to be part of the political-military-economic fiasco you call society.

Like the Indian's Hemp Drug Commission three-quarters of a century earlier, the Canadian Le Dain Commission conducted an inquiry into the use of marijuana. On page 156 of the report is the following:

"In the case of cannabis, the positive points which are claimed for it include the following:

• It is a relaxant;

• It is disinhibiting;

• It increases self-confidence and the feeling of creativity (whether justified by objective results or not);

• It increases sensual awareness and appreciation;

• It facilitates self-acceptance and in this way makes it easier to accept others;

• It serves a sacramental function in promoting a sense of spiritual community among users;

• It is a shared pleasure;

• Because it is illicit and the object of strong disapproval from those who are, by and large, opposed to social change, it is a symbol of protest and a means of strengthening the sense of identity among those who are strongly critical of certain aspects of our society and value structure today."

On page 144 of the Report, marijuana is associated with peace.

> "In our conversation [with students and young people], they have frequently contrasted marijuana and alcohol effects to describe the former as a drug of peace, a drug that reduces tendencies to aggression, while suggesting that the latter drug produces hostile and aggressive behavior. Thus marijuana is seen as particularly appropriate to a generation that emphasizes peace and is, in many ways, anti-competitive."

A research finding, much publicized in the past few years, shows the usage of marijuana may decrease blood levels of the male hormone testosterone in men. Again, there are contradictory experiments, and the issue is not settled. Of course, even if marijuana does have this effect, its significance is not clear. High testosterone levels may correlate more with aggressiveness than with sexual adjustment; some men in our society might benefit from a reduction in this hormone.

In a magazine article by G.S. Chopra entitled "Man and Marijuana" there is a section dealing with Human Experiments. One hundred persons with an established marijuana smoking habit, smoked marijuana. They described some of the symptoms as follows:

"I have done things today which I usually dislike but which I rather enjoyed doing today."

"Nothing seemed impossible to accomplish."

"I assumed a cool and composed attitude and forgot all mental worries."

"It relieves the sense of fatigue and gives rise to feelings of happiness."

"I feel like laughing."

"I feel like taking more food."

"The world is gay around me."

"I feel inclined to work."

"I am a friend to all and have no enemy in the world."

In Tales of Hashish, Francois Lallemand describes hashish as follows:

"The most constant and remarkable property of hashish is to exalt the dominant ideas of the person who has taken it; to make him see in the clearest way his most complicated plans come to fruition without difficulty; his dearest projects realized without obstacle; to furnish him with the precise intuition he seeks. Finally, it lets him taste in thought the absolute possession of everything according to his wishes and habitual passions; and according to the direction of his thoughts at the moment, the hashish acts on him. This is what explains the different effects one hears spoken of, because the effects greatly vary according to the individual and his momentary disposition."

Also in Tales of Hashish:

"Our soldiers on the Egyptian Expedition, deprived of all communication with France, began to take it despite the standing orders of the chief general. But what do you want? It's the sovereign remedy for melancholy, discouragement, and every kind of disappointment. I thought I would still need it in France for some time to come, and that is why I brought back an ample provision, and I offer you some of it. Try it, even if only out of curiosity. What risk is there? A small dose, a single cup of this precious infusion can give you only gaiety and consolation. Your most delightful wishes will become transformed, for the moment, into realities: you will possess the gift of second sight; you will be raised to the rank of prophets."

Quotes from *Psychedelics Encyclopedia* by Peter Stafford, copyright 1977:

"Ken Kesey, who nowadays feels reluctant to recommend any other mental drug due to the impurities one might encounter, provides the ultimate pot commercial: 'But good old grass I can recommend. To be just without being mad...to be peaceful without being stupid; to be interested without being compulsive; to be happy without being hysterical...smoke grass.'"

CHAPTER 20
"INSPIRATION"

The core of the matter is that most users of cannabis find it inspiring in many ways. They claim that it not only heightens sexual feelings, but it inspires religious feelings, increases creativity, helps solve problems, get in touch with themselves, and expand the scope of their minds. Even rats, when given a diet of THC have been shown to be capable of learning how to run mazes faster than when they're left *unstoned*.

The point of all this is that when people talk about marijuana adding a third dimension to pictures, or new depths to colors or creating "synesthesia," i.e., where the auditory becomes visual, they are merely discussing a few changes in normal external perception. Distortions in the sense of time and space are fascinating. More to the point of the drug's eventual effect upon humanity are those effects which come under the headings of "insight," or "inspiration."

To drive the point home, allow one more listing from the Tart materials. (Probably the most relevant study to date about what might be considered "typical" pot experience is the one made by Dr. Charles Tart, reported in his book ON BEING STONED [Science and Behavior Books].

The following is what appeared as common experience among marijuana users:

Skip intermediate steps in problem-solving Insights into others

Thoughts more intuitive

Ideas more original

Converse intelligently, even though things were forgotten

Learn a lot about what makes people tick

Say more profound, appropriate things

Intuitive, empathic, understanding of people

Sexual love union of souls as well as bodies

Inhibitions lowered

Mind feels more efficient in problem-solving

At one with the world

Events, actions become archetypal

    Before leaving the topic of marijuana's mental effects, a word should be added about its ability to give access to long-buried memories, to facilitate rapport and to aid psychotherapeutic "transference." Let me cite the experience of Dr. Harry Harmon, of how he first became interested in the use of this drug to expedite psychotherapy. He had been treating a patient without much success for some time...when, on a particular occasion, the information he had been seeking in vain to elicit for some time suddenly began to flow forth freely. Harmon was astonished. He asked his patient what was different this time. His patient informed him that he had come in *stoned*.

    "Stoned?" said Dr. Harmon, "What is this 'stoned?'"And thus, Dr. Harmon soon came to realize how this weed could unblock a person's mind, an insight which launched him into an entirely different phase of his therapy and life.

    While Gautier and his literary colleagues were exploring the romance of these feelings, another small club of Frenchmen was using dosages of hashish ten-times greater to follow the soul's ecstatic journey out of the body into a spiritual world. Under the tutelage of psycho-pharmacologist Louis-Alphonse Cahagnet, these subjects documented visions of death and the afterlife experiences identical to those known as "near-death experiences." The prototypical experience started with the user being pulled out of time into a sacred stillness. A feeling of peace and a sense of well-being captured the soul as it separated from the body, then flung it into a bright light at a moment of supreme happiness.

    "Geometrically sculpted images introduce themes of cosmic importance. The forms parade across the mind's eye so fast that the cherubs melt into gargoyles, then a crypt of one's own body. The blue geometric forms become towering cathedrals filled with the white light of the Universal Being."

When Cahagnet's subjects explored the beyond within, their outward behavior had been identical to that of the animals receiving high doses of hashish or THC: quiet and still, almost mesmerized. While we may never know what else birds and monkeys see besides blue geometric patterns, their cannabis experiences may very well reflect the same joy and happiness that characterizes human intoxications. After all, we share the same drive and pursuit for the drug, even similar brain mechanisms – so why shouldn't the experiences created by such common biology be alike?

Darwin viewed laughter as a counterpart to discomfort, a way in which the species communicates a state of well-being. Konrad Lorenz saw it as an expression of social unity, a way to thwart aggression. The pursuit of the taming and comforting effects of intoxication from hemp seeds and other mild forms of Cannabis might just be the animal kingdom's way of trying to laugh.

Recent psychopharmacological studies have discovered THC (active ingredients of marijuana) has its own unique receptor sites in the brain, indicating man and marijuana have a precultural relationship. (Jack Herer; "The Emperor Wears No Clothes.")

In the article *The Chemistry of Reefer Madness* (OMNI Magazine August 1989) Miles Herkenham is quoted saying of the marijuana brain button:

"What really struck me was the front-brain loading. It's sort of a high-brow receptor. The binding sites are incredibly numerous compared with other neurotransmitter systems, which suggests they are receptors for an important, ubiquitous transmitter."

Taken from the article *Marijuana: The Symbol and the Ritual*, by U. Ballante of the Psychology Department of the San Francisco State College (Journal of Secondary Education, May 1968, Vol. 43, No. 5).

The time we live in also has an effect on the current upswing of marijuana use. Does the current milieu require, and yet lack, a ceremonial activity to bring people back together; not just physically, but in such a way as to yield a real feeling of interpersonal relatedness and connectedness?

In his fictional work, Heinlein describes a water ritual used by the inhabitants of Mars. Upon sharing water together, the people become bound eternally to one another as profound friends. They become, in effect, "soul brothers." The contention here is that marijuana use may fulfill the need for such a ritualistic binding.

Previously, our culture did not lack ritualistic gatherings. It was not long ago that our churches still yielded mystery, meaning and vitality. It was not until recently that the church, in its attempt to hold onto its position and form, began to be widely perceived by the intellectual elite as a "denial of life, a denial of God, a denial of the Spirit."

But the church was not the only source of ritualistic vitality. Competing with the church and surpassing it as a widespread source of envitalized ritual was the state. What the hour in church on Sunday no longer accomplished for the individual, the Pledge of Allegiance and the National Anthem did.

It is absolutely essential for the individual, no matter how intellectually oriented, to have moving experiences which relate him to other people and to a higher moral order. Ritual is one of the primary keys to this kind of experience.

It must be realized that simply carrying out a series of common actions does not establish a state of ritual. Ritual cannot be detached from its ends. It is only when the series of actions yields a derived sense of personal interrelatedness and a sense of moral connectedness that the pattern of action can be designated as a ritual. Should these effects cease, there is no longer ritual; there is no longer meaning.

For many, if not most, the rituals of the church and state can no longer function as rituals. Not many are any longer profoundly moved, at least positively, by the Pledge of Allegiance or the National Anthem.

We are in the process of building up an argument which, moreover, perceives marijuana as an instrument of historical forces, rather than as a significant entity of itself. If marijuana were not so readily available and ideally suited to fill the needs and void of the times, something else would have been seized upon or created.

Since marijuana is a physiologically rather innocuous drug, because its effects are readily influenced by the environment, because it has a history rich in mystery, because it exists principally outside the system, and, most of all, because it has a nature and tradition ideally suited for a highly social "happening," marijuana has become the focal point and symbol for solving a most urgent historical crisis. This crisis is none other than <u>man's separation from his fellowman, and, just as disastrous, his separation from himself</u>.

The highly social nature of marijuana is unmistakable; one of the most striking features of the drug is that marijuana is rarely consumed alone. For a variety of reasons, but particularly because of its adaptability to a social ritual, marijuana is almost always consumed in the form of smoking. It is passed from hand to hand, making the elements of sharing and giving central and crucial to the experience.

The setting of the situation also tends to promote a feeling of being relaxed and comfortable. A typical setting will find the people sitting on the floor in a circular fashion. A refreshing gentleness tends to pervade the atmosphere. Flickering candles, the mellow and often child-like facial expressions, music—all tend to contribute to the sensation of peace.

It is not unusual to seek out a natural environment in which to "turn on." The beaches, parks, and woods are frequent choices. No matter what the choice of setting, the intent and preference is to seek out a place of relative peace and beauty. This choice of setting has much to do with the derived effects.

Marijuana is also a form of social offering. To refuse it in such a situation, is to turn down one of the few remaining instances where people still reach out to one another.

The social component of ritual is more than amply satisfied by the circumstances surrounding and encompassing marijuana smoking. <u>The direct goal of the marijuana ritual in distinction to traditional ritual seems to be the strengthening and elation of personal ties.</u>

For example, in rituals of initiation, the direct goal of the ceremony is to pave the way for the assimilation of the adolescent into the role of the adult. Here, the general bonds of the tribal members are strengthened only indirectly by virtue of participating in a common and deeply meaningful ritualistic ceremony. In contrast, the positive marijuana ritual not only receives the benefit of this indirect boost to social connectedness, but also, the ritual directs the aim of the activity itself towards this principal end – the bringing of people together.

It must be recalled that there is nothing inherent in marijuana that can make people subjectively feel closer. Granted, there are certain predisposing qualities, such as its peculiar history, "wickedness," availability, and ambiguity of effects, that make marijuana an ideal rallying ground for a social "happening." However, one must look to the total encompassing atmosphere surrounding marijuana smoking to actually account for its generally positive social effects.

So far we have pointed out the highly social and ceremonial aspects of marijuana smoking. Earlier we designated one additional factor that is crucial to defining a state of ritual. We mentioned that the activity must serve as a basis for linking the individual up with a higher moral order. Another way of stating the same thing is that the ceremony must serve to kindle positive and optimistic forces in the individual.

To the extent that church ritual still survives for particular individuals, the above kind of transcending effect is obvious. In addition, it must be realized that when "The State" is the ritualistic source, there is this highly moral and transcending quality.

However, in this situation, the State takes over the function of God. It is The State that is perceived as the source and promoter of a higher moral order. Instead of linking oneself with God, the individual links himself up with The State. Psychologically, the same process is taking place when THE STATE is no longer viewed as morally perfect; when the shade of gray supersedes the black and white, and then the influence of the State is reduced as a source of ritual.

One way in which the total marijuana smoking environment seems to prompt a transcendental experience is by seemingly generating a state of increased aesthetic awareness. Sometimes it appears to be more than a simple kindling of increased awareness of nature and beauty. At these moments, the intensity seems to become so great that one no longer senses a distinction between one's self and nature. A certain continuity of experience is affected.

In another manner, the marijuana environment seems capable of extending feelings beyond the people immediately present. Frequently, a person will not only experience profound warmth for the people around him, but will simultaneously feel a deep-rooted connectedness to a much larger group. Sometimes the sensation extends to the whole subgroup, sometimes encompasses all of humanity, and sometimes, in that most cherished instance, embraces the entire cosmos...

CHAPTER 21
"MARIJUANA AS THE EUCHARIST"

According to the Encyclopedia Britannica, in the section on *Roman Catholicism*:

> "To understand the meaning and use of the Eucharist, we must see it as an act of universal worship, of cooperation, of association; else it loses the greater part of its significance. Neither in Roman Catholic nor in Protestant Eucharistic practice does the sacrament retain much of the symbolism of Christian unity, which it clearly has. Originally, the symbolism was that of a community throughout the whole of human culture."

History has shown that marijuana has been used as a sacrifice, a sacrament, a ritual fumigant (incense), a good-will offering, and as a means of communing with the divine spirit. It has been used to seal treaties, friendships, and solemn, binding agreements and to legitimize covenants. It has been used as a traditional defense against evil and in purification. It has been used in divinations (1. the art or practice that seeks to foresee or foretell future events or discover hidden knowledge; 2. unusual insight; intuitive perception). It has been used in remembrance of the dead and in ancestor worship. It has been used and praised for its medicinal properties. It has been used for food, clothing, fuel, paper, oil, sails, cord, fish-nets and relaxation.

Most Christians agree that participation in the Eucharist is supposed to enhance and deepen communion of believers not only with Christ, but also with one another. We must, therefore, ask the question, "What substance did the ancients use as a community meal to facilitate communion with one another and with the Lord?" The answer to that question is marijuana. Hemp as originally used in religious ritual, temple activities, and tribal rites involved groups of worshippers rather than the solitary individual. The pleasurable psychoactive effects were then, as now, communal experiences.

Practically every major religion and culture of the ancient world utilized marijuana as part of their religious observance. Marijuana was the ambrosia of the ancient world. It was the food, drink, and perfume of the gods. It was used by the Hindus, the Buddhist, the Taoist, the Shinto, the Moslems and the Zoroastrian religions. It was used by the Africans, the Egyptians, the Assyrians, the Asians, the Europeans, and possibly the Indians of the Americas. Would it be too much to suggest that the ancient Israelites also utilized marijuana?

When one undertakes the study of the world's religions, they find an undertone of truth that resonates with the same vibration through all of them. Yet because so many people are up to their knees in dogma, religion has become the catalyst for many a war. There is a Sufi tale, by the poet Rumi, which illustrates this. It tells of some men who stumble upon an elephant in the dark. Each man sought to examine the Elephant by touch alone (from one perspective); each thought that the one part they examined was the total reality of the object. For one, the elephant was only a fan (ear); for another, a rope (tail); for a third, a pillar (a leg); and so on. They all failed to understand the whole elephant and were therefore lost in bickering about its true identity.

CHAPTER 22
"MARIJUANA AS THE TREE OF LIFE"

Rev. 22:2 *"On each side of the river (of life) stood the tree of life, bearing twelve crops of fruit, yielding its fruit every month. And the leaves of the tree are for the healing of the Nations."*

Hemp burning censers, used by the ancient Scythians, were found in Western Alta. Also at the site, a large felt rug was found. The rug had the repeated design of a horseman approaching the Great Goddess, who holds the "Tree of Life" in one hand.

The following was taken from the "Keys of St. Peter," written in 1867 by E.D. Bunsen:

"The records of the 'Tree of Life' are the sublimest proofs of the unity and continuity of tradition, and of its Eastern tradition, and of its Eastern origin. The earliest records of the most ancient Oriental tradition refer to a 'Tree of Life' which was guarded by spirits. The juice of the fruit of this sacred tree, like the tree itself, was called Soma in Sanscrit and Haoma in Zend; it was revered as the life preserving essence."

In Genesis 3:24 "God placed Cherubims (angels of Man: read chapter entitled MAN AN ANGEL) and a flaming sword which turned every way, to keep the way of the 'Tree of Life.' " In Psalms 104:4 and Hebrews 1:7 "God maketh his angels spirits; his ministers a flaming fire."

There are many common threads that include the "Tree of Life" found in the various cultures around the world. Some of the other common things include the story of Adam and Eve in the Garden of Eden, the story of the flood, and the burning of incense and marijuana for religious purposes. These common traditions indicate that they spread from a common source. That source was the Garden of Eden.

We of the Ethiopian Zion Coptic Church declare that that source was Ethiopia (all of Africa at one time was referred to as Ethiopia) and that civilization came down the River Nile to Egypt, on to Mesopotamia, on to India and China and Europe and right on around the world.

NEWSWEEK SEPT. 23, 1991:

"*Black Americans were robbed of their history. Now they are reclaiming it for future generations.*

"*If you visited the Smithsonian's National Museum of Natural History last week, you would have found that the second-floor Physical Anthropology galleries housing the reconstruction of the head of the proto-human Australopithecus have been closed. Visitors are not permitted to view the exhibit until curators prepare a new head, which, in accordance with current scientific thinking on the origins of humanity, will look quite different from the one that has been on display since 1966. It will be black.*

"*The Smithsonians are negotiating over exactly when in the last 200,000 years white people joined the parade of humanity.*

"*Afrocentrism: a view in which Europeans and their white descendants no longer occupy the central and exalted position. African people for 500 years have lived on the intellectual terms of Europeans. The African perspective has finally come to dinner. [It's time for the world to learn the truth that's been hidden from their "wise"]*

"*Afrocentrism brilliantly exposes how whites have manipulated history and ethnography for their own advantage. In Europe, racist scholars obliterated the influence of whole African civilizations... Bolstering the case of slavery. Worldwide intellectual apartheid.*"

Down through the ages, and now seven times more (because of technology), the ruling class, all of them lumped together in the United Nations; the Popes and all the wicked, have set up what looks like a caring, sharing, loving principality (not that there aren't streaks of good, basically good ones, and even truly good ones, yet I speak of the prophetic, eternal words), one that is "the best we humans have to offer." Yet they never take into account the excluded ones ("when the wicked rule, a man [the man of Truth] is hidden"). Not that they hide, yet they are consciously hidden from the world by the powers that be.

The majority of the people in most places (especially the U.S.) do not vote; therefore, those in power are not there due to the majority rule, yet simply the majority of those that came to the polls (sometimes less than 30%).

George Washington said that if the people weren't satisfied, they should erect a new government. Nevertheless, most can't find a superior, and those that can, can't stand up for fear of the "lion's den" and the "fiery furnace."

NEWSWEEK CONTINUED:

"*Afrocentrism contains within it an uncomfortable truth.*" [*White racism and the "Jewish" are focal points in the charade of stolen ethnography. Who are the real Jews? And who are those that Christ calls the Synagogue of Satan? They are not Jews, though they call themselves so; what actually happened is that the blacks, the origin of the Semitic Jews, fought against their prophets, and the Assyrians, who are the same Jewish people now. They came into Israel, and stole the Ark of the Covenant, and all the teachings of the true deity. Hence, we have a counterfeit, and the real. This also began the enslavement of the black race for six thousand years and 'Is-rael' being in bondage to the worldly powers, as the prophecy declares. For if these Jewish people, who are free, were genuine, then according to the prophesy, their king and savior would be reigning with them.*]

KRS-One, a modern musical group, pays homage to that great black religious leader Jesus Christ.

NEWSWEEK CONTINUED:

"What is school if it doesn't build Children's self-confidence? American education does that for white children. From the day white kids walk into school, they are told that they are heirs to the greatest achievements of humankind. Are they not by definition universal?

"The blacks reclaim Egypt, which in their view was stolen from Africa and relocated in the 'Mideast' by 19th-century scholars who couldn't bear to think that Africans built the Pyramids. They assert that much of the culture and technology associated with ancient Greece was actually Egyptian, transplanted to the Aegean by conquest and settlement. They view the intellectual history of the West as one frantic effort to deny this truth. (Minor irony: when Europeans forcibly impose their culture on a conquered people, it's called "imperial"-ism.)

They're not against anybody. It's just where you take your stand.

"If you go back far enough, [not the monkey, for I believe that proof of pre-historic civilized man is just hidden from their wise. For what about Atlantis, etc] we are all Afrocentrists.

"They didn't dispute the achievements of the great black kingdoms of West Africa in governance, social organization and economic sophistication. But they dismissed them as a sideshow in human civilization. 'And even if Egypt was pretty great...well, Egypt was not really Africa.' Just as Africans were taken out of Africa, so Egypt has been taken out of Africa.

"The classicists were racists and anti-Semites. Most modern researchers say 'there's no real question' that 19th-century academics were racist and anti-Semitic.

"Greek historians wrote that such great lawgivers as Lykourgos studied in Egypt and brought back the legal and political basis for the West's politics.

"The answer is as plain as the Sphinx's face.

"Almost all scholars agree: For seven thousand years Egypt has been populated by African, Asian and Mediterranean peoples. 'It was a thoroughly mixed population [one body, we, one Ethiopian doctrine, one in charity) that got darker and more Negroid the further up you went'...

"It was not too many years ago that anthropologists desperately sought to trace humankind's origins to anywhere but Africa. That debate has been settled in favor of an east African genesis [civilization came down the River Nile], a resolution that struck at the heart of European biological arrogance. They have clearly forced scholars to re-examine the roots of Western civilization.

"One cannot argue that there is no difference—or that difference necessarily means hostility. One may be alien and yet not hostile.

"Can't deny personal histories. What's known must be taught."

The idea of the Edenic happiness of the first human beings constitutes one of the universal traditions. Among the Egyptians, the terrestrial reign of the god Ra, who inaugurated the existence of the world and of human life, was a golden age to which they continually looked back with regret and envy. It's like it has never been seen since. (*Bible Myths and Their Parallels in Other Religions* by T.N. Boane copyright 1882 - reprinted 1985 pg. 10.)

Dr. Kglisch, writing of the Garden of Eden, says: "The paradise is no exclusive feature of the early history of the Hebrews. Most of the ancient nations have similar narratives about a happy abode, which care does not approach, and which re-echoes with the sounds of the purest bliss." (Com. on the Old Testament. vol. i, p.70)

The ancient Greek boasted of their Golden Age when sorrow and trouble were not known. An ancient Grecian poet describes it thus:

"Men lived like Gods, without vices or passions, vexations or toil. In happy companionship with divine beings, they passed their days in tranquility and joy, living together in perfect equality, united by mutual confidence and love. The earth was more beautiful than now, and spontaneously yielded an abundant variety of fruits. Human beings and animals spoke the same language and conversed with each other. Men were considered mere boys at a hundred years old. They had none of the infirmities of age to trouble them, and when they passed to regions of superior life, it was in a gentle slumber."

The Chinese have their Age of Virtue when nature furnished abundant food, and man lived peacefully, surrounded by all the beasts. In their sacred books, there is a story concerning a mysterious garden, where grew a tree bearing "apples of immortality," guarded by a winged serpent, called a Dragon. They describe a primitive age of the world when the earth yielded abundance of delicious fruits without cultivation, and the seasons were untroubled by wind and storms. There was no calamity, sickness, or death. Men were then good without effort, for the human heart was in harmony with the peacefulness and beauty of nature. (*Bible Myths and Their Parallels in Other Religions*, pg. 14)

The ancient Egyptians had their legend of the "Tree of Life." It is mentioned in their sacred books that Osiris ordered the names of some souls to be "written on this "Tree of Life." The fruit of which made those who ate it to become as gods. (Prog. Relig. Ideas, vol. i. p. 159)

As mentioned earlier, among the most ancient traditions of the Hindus is that of the "Tree of Life," called Soma in Sanskrit and Haoma in Zend, the juice of which imparted immortality. This most wonderful tree was guarded by spirits. (see Bunsens Keys of St. Peter, pg. 414)

Mircea Eliade, perhaps one of the foremost authorities on the history of religions, states of the Haoma (which he believes to be marijuana) in his *History of Religious Ideas, Vol. l.* the following:

"Now Haoma is rich in xvarenah, the sacred fluid, at once igneous, luminous, vivifying, and spermatic. Ahura Mazda (the Supreme Zoroastrian deity) is pre-eminently the possessor of xvarenah, but this name also springs from the forehead of Mithra (the Magi refers to Mithra as the Eucharist of the Lord and Savior, the second person in their Trinity), and like a solar light, emanates from the heads of sovereigns. However, every human being possesses his xvarenah, and on the day or transfiguration, i.e., of the final renovation, the great light seeming to come from the body will burn continually on this earth."

This xvarenah is much the same as the Hindu "Eye of Shiva," which every human has, to some extent. In the Bible, just after the verse on the tree of life, we find mention of a similar light to this xvarenah. Revelation 22: 4-5:

"They will see his face, and his name will be in their foreheads. There will be no more night; they will not need the light or a lamp or the light of the sun, for the Lord God will give them light."

It is of interest to note that both the Bible and Zend-Avesta describe the light or xvarenah as emanating from within the forehead. The human brain has its own unique THC receptor sites, as shown in a previous chapter. According to Miles who was quoted in an article on the THC receptor sites, appearing in the August 1989 issue of Omni Magazine, said: "What really struck me was the front brain loading. It is sort of a high brow receptor. The binding sites are numerous compared with other neurotransmitter systems, which suggests they are receptors for an important, ubiquitous [Omnipresent - existing or being everywhere at the same time] transmitter."

Researchers at the National Institute of Mental Health (NIMH) have identified a naturally occurring chemical in the body that binds to the cannabinoid receptors found just two years ago. The newly discovered compound is being named anandamide, from anande, the Sanskrit word for bliss (notice how they hide the truth—BLISS, using a word no one knows, like anandamide!). The New York Times, Tuesday, December 22nd, 1992 c-8: Bliss is defined as 1. Complete happiness 2. Heaven, paradise. Only agents of Satan could fight against such a concept.

The ancient Egyptians had a word to designate the "third eye," the uraeus, related in old tradition to the pineal body and to the spirit. Perhaps modern science has discovered what the ancients knew – that man has a third eye or spiritual eye, and that marijuana can play a part in opening this eye.

Zoroastrian, alchemical, and occult literature often refer to connecting with your higher self as marrying your Goddess. A 15th century Monk, Bachelor of Medicine and author of the French literary classic "Gargantua& Pantagruel," Francois Rabelais, ended a chapter on hemp, which he referred to as "the herb pantagruelion" with references to this spiritual marriage. Rabelais was temporarily imprisoned in his convent when he and another brother started studying Greek works which opened up the original New Testament.

Rabelais managed to obtain an indult from Pope Clement VII and went on to write his famous books. Unfortunately, little is known of Rabelais after the release of his works, he virtually disappeared under the outrage from the Church and the *State* over their publication.

Rabelais gives an excellent Botanical description of hemp:

"These leaves are in equal and parallel distances spread around the stalk, by the number in every rank of five or seven"; and he goes on to give descriptions of its uses:

> *"All the cotton plants of Tylos on the Persian Gulf, of Arabia and Malta have not dressed so many people as this plant alone... it protects armies against cold and rain much more effectively than did the skin tents of old... By it*

bows are strung...slings made...shapes and makes serviceable boots, leggings, shoes, slippers."

Rabelais ends a chapter on hemp with the following quote:

> "And marry our Goddesses; which is their one means of rising to be Gods. In the end, they decided to deliberate on a means of preventing this and called a council."

I am of the opinion that the council Rabelais refers to is the formation of the Roman Catholic Church when sects like the Gnostics and Essenes were wiped out or driven underground. And the marriage to the Goddess referred to, is the marriage of the higher self, the marriage of the left side of the brain with the right.

In the New Testament's Timothy 4:3-5, we can find mention of this marriage and prohibition: "*Forbidding certain marriages and commanding to abstain from meats which God hath created to be received with thanksgiving of them which believe and know the truth.*"

In Genesis 1, it states, "*I have given you every herb bearing seed which is upon the face of the Earth, and every tree, in which is the fruit of a tree yielding seed, to you it shall be for meat.*"

It is also in Genesis, where we first find mention of the *Tree of Life*, here it states, "who ever shall eat from the fruit of this tree shall live for ever." The fruit of hemp is its seed and as I am sure many readers are aware, the hemp seed is the best source of Essential Fatty Acids. In a new book by seven-time Nobel Prize Nominee, Dr. Johanna Budwig "Flax Oil as a True Aid Against Arthritis, Heart Cancer, and Other Diseases," research indicates that a balanced diet of Essential Fatty Acids would keep our cells biologically electron rich. Saturated fats, which make up the vast majority of the food oils we now use, alter the electronic charge of the unsaturated cell membrane, decreasing the cells ability to store and receive electrons from the Sun." Budwig goes on to quote Quantum physicist Dessauer as stating, "If it were possible to increase the concentration of solar electrons tenfold in this biological electron rich molecule, man would live to be 10,000 years old."

In certain rites, both in the Indian and the Parsee religions, the devotees drink the juice of the Soma or Haoma plant. They consider it a god as well as a plant... Says Mr. Baring-Gould:

"*Among the ancient Hindus, Soma was a chief deity; he is called 'the Giver of Life' and of the 'Protector,' he who is 'the Guide to Immortality.' He became incarnate among man, was taken by them and slain, and brayed in a mortar. But he rose in flame to heaven, to be the 'Benefactor of the World,' and the Mediator between God and Man.*

"Through communion with him in his sacrifice, man, (who partook of this god), has an assurance of immortality, for by that sacrament he obtains union with his divinity." (Baring-Gould; Orig. Relig. Belief, vol. l. pg.401)

In the book "Persephone's Quest," by J. Ott, R.G. Wasson, C. Ruck, and Stella Kramrisch, there is a description of the Mahavira Vessel and the Plant Putika given by Kramrisch. Miss Kramrisch gives good evidence linking the identity of Putika with Soma and goes on to give a description of how it was prepared in the Mahavira Vessel. The vessel consists of three pots, which are placed one inside of the other. The clay of the innermost one is mixed with several ingredients, among them, the plant Putika (Soma), the pots are then placed on a fire and heated to a glow. At this stage, milk is poured into the innermost one and the resulting curds were consumed by the worshipper.

THC, the main psycho-active ingredient of marijuana, is oil based. If you consider hemp to be Putika, then the water based clay, when heated, would push out the oil-based cannabis resins into the milk, which is fat based, and an intoxicating beverage would result. Miss Kramrisch goes on to state of the Putika, "The plant Putika, however, when laid on the fire as an offering, is said to become fragrant; it acquires the odor of sanctity."

The Magi were the founders of magnetism. In fact, both the words magic and magnet are derived from Magi. Hemp is one of only two hypnotics (the second is the going under phase of chloroform), and as the work of Anton Mesmer has shown, there is a correlation between magnetism and hypnotism.

One of the few surviving Zoroastrian Holy Books, the "Vendidad," gives a description of two mortals, who upon drinking Soma, are transported in soul to heaven, to have the highest mysteries revealed to them. In Ronald K. Siegel's book "Intoxication," we find mention of psychopharmacologist Louis-Alphonse Cahagnet, who, in the mid-1800s, conducted research with very large doses of hashish. He documented his subject's visions of death and afterlife. These visions were identical with those we now know of as "near death experiences." Further mention of Cahagnet's research can be found in Colin Wilson's "Afterlife."

In addition, the Soma was something done often with consistent results. 12,000 years of human experience with cannabis shows that it can be done often with consistent results.

The Soma of the ancient Hindus was undoubtedly a hemp drink. After all, their whole culture and religion revolved around the hemp plant. Hemp was a giver of life and health. It was a Protector; it was a guide to Immortality. It was a mediator between God and man. It was a Benefactor to the world. By that sacrament, mankind could obtain union with his divinity.

In Hindu mythology, Amrita means immortality; likewise, the ambrosial drink which produced it. Tradition maintains that when nectar or Amrita dropped from heaven cannabis sprouted (from it).

Early Indian legends maintained that the angel of mankind lived in the leaves of the hemp plant – It was so sacred. It was reputed to deter evil and cleanse its user of sin. It was able to give its visions of the gods. It was referred to as gods' food and Shiva's plant. Shiva was the Supreme God of many Hindu sects.

The quote from the Keys of St. Peter mentions the Haoma of the Zend-Avesta, (the Zoroastrian holy book). Dr. M. Aldrich, an authority on marijuana has declared a belief that this Haoma was a hemp beverage. Mircea Eliade, one of the foremost authorities on the history of religions, shared this belief. One reason for this is perhaps because, in the Zend-Avesta, hemp occupies the first place in a list of 10,000 medicinal plants. We have already noted, in Egypt and India, hemp was made into a drink. In India, it was the drink of the Gods and was associated with immortality.

We have noted the use of marijuana as incense amongst the Assyrians in the 7th or 8th century before Christ. We have cited that at Babylon, "The glorious gods smell the incense, noble of heaven; pure wine, which no hand had touched, do they enjoy." Like their Babylonian neighbors to the west, we have noted that the most important of the ancient Indian gods was Agni, the god of fire, who like the Babylonian god, Girru-Nusku, acted as a messenger between men and the gods. The fire (Agni) upon the altar was regarded as a messenger, their invoker.

It was been shown that in China, marijuana was burned as incense which was a means of achieving immortality. We have provided evidence that Hemp was a symbol of power over evil and in Shen Nung pharmacopeia was known as the liberator of sin. The Chinese believed that the legendary Shen Nung first taught the cultivation of hemp in the 28th century B.C.; so highly regarded was Shen Nung that he was deified. Today, he is regarded as the Father of Chinese Medicine. Shen Nung was also regarded as the Lord of Fire and he sacrificed on Tai Shan, a mountain of hoary antiquity.

It is logical to assume that mankind first discovered the properties of marijuana by first eating it. Later it was made into a drink, and also burnt.

In Genesis 3: 24 God placed Cherubims (angels) and a flaming sword which turned every way, to keep the way of the *Tree of Life*. In Psalms 104: 4 and Hebrews 1 God maketh his angels spirits: his ministers a flaming fire. In Revelations, it is declared that Man is the angel.

From the time Adam had to leave the garden, the holy ones had to keep the way of the Tree *of Life*, even against an encompassing army. Through the Old Testament until Christ, as the genealogy in the beginning of Matthew states, from God to his son Adam to Christ was a line (spiritual line), of man to man – A father-son adoption covenant: Man and his spiritual generation, keeping the way of the *Tree of Life*. There has always been a high priest of Melchizedek: Jes-us. In other words, there has always been a prophet that has kept the truth alive. The truth cannot be killed.

In the Nag Hammadi Library, Sophia's (who is the female personification of wisdom) daughter turns herself into a tree to hide from the authorities. In Jamaica today marijuana is known as the "Tree of Life" and the "Weed of Wisdom."

In the Nag Hammadi's Apocalypse of Peter (Gnostic scripture), Jesus prophesies on modern day Christianity:

> *"They will cleave to the name of a dead man, thinking that they will become pure. But they will become greatly defiled and they will fall into the hand of an evil, cunning man and a manifold dogma, and they will be ruled heretically; for some will say evil things against each other... But many others, who oppose the truth and are the*

messengers of error, will set up their error and their law against these pure thoughts of mine, as looking out from one (perspective), thinking that good and evil are from one (source). They do business in my word... And there shall be others of those who are outside our number who name themselves bishops and also deacons, as if they have received their authority from God. They bend themselves under the judgement of the leaders. These people are dry canals."

The following is from the Gospel According To Thomas (translated from Coptic Texts):

"Joshua says: 'If those who lead you say to you: Behold, the Kingdom is in the sky, then the birds of the sky will precede you. If they say to you: it is in the sea, then the fish will precede you. But the Kingdom is within you and it is without you. If you know that, you are the Sons of the Living Father. But if you do not know yourselves, then you are in poverty and you are poverty."

Heaven is not outside of man. Hell is not outside of man. The heavenly people are those who store up virtue, charity and morality in their hearts. The hellish people are those who are:

"...filled with all unrighteousness, fornication, wickedness, covetousness, maliciousness; full of envy, murder, debate, deceit, malignity; whisperers, backbiters, haters of God, despiteful, proud, boasters, inventors of evil things, disobedient to parents, without understanding, covenant breakers, without natural affection, implacable, unmerciful: Who knowing the judgment of God, that they which commit such things are worthy of death, not only do the same, but have pleasure in them that do them." (Romans 1:29-32)

It is interesting to note that the Egyptians have at various times brutally suppressed those who used marijuana. At one point in time, they even wrenched the teeth out of those who used it.

Egypt, along with South Africa, led the international fight (in the League of Nations which is now called the United Nations) to have cannabis outlawed worldwide. Egypt was where the Coptic Church was founded.

It is the churches belief that when Mystery Babylon (false

religion, politics, and commerce) falls, the *Tree of Life* will be the mainstay of the remnant – Not just for prayer and communion, but for food, clothing and shelter as well as providing necessary oxygen for replenishing the ozone layer.

Should mankind fall so low as to bring on God's fiery judgment; through the use of nuclear weapons, marijuana has proven its usefulness in the treatment of radiation sickness. This remarkable plant is truly for the healing of the nations. Note the following 1992 article by two medical doctors at UCLA:

Researchers at UCLA Discover Hemp Seed's Essential Oils By Wm M.D. & R Lee Hamilton, MD. UCLA

"It's no longer a matter of ignorance versus politics. There is no time left to argue. We have reached a turning point and we must intervene now if we are to have a world left to live in. The truth must be known. The insane prohibitions against the most valuable plant on earth, cannabis hemp, must yield to public demand and hopefully soon.

"The promise of super health and the possibility of feeding the world is at our fingertips.

"The applications for the wonder plant hemp are continually being discovered and re-discovered. Food, housing, fuel, clothing, paper, shoes, etc., to name a few.

"Medical applications are well researched and documented. Studies from Harvard and UCLA Medical schools are specific and have positive findings using cannabis in medical intervention in many applications."

Studies by Dr. Johanna Budwig, M.D. (nominated for the prize every year since 1979) have shown unparalleled results in the use of essential fatty acids in the treatment of terminal cancer patients. What are essential fatty acids? The term essential is the tip off. Truly, there can be no life anywhere without the essential oils. These essential oils support the immune system and guard against viral and other insults to the immune system. Studies are in progress using the essential oils to support the immune systems of HIV-positive patients. So far, they have been extremely promising.

What is the richest source of the essential oils? Yes, you guessed it – the seeds from the cannabis hemp plant. They contain

25% LNA acid, and 51% LA acid. What better proof of the life-giving values of the now illegal seed.

Fortunately, when the Creator made the hemp plant, there were no politicians and lobbies for multinational corporations around to advise, and no ignorant congressional committees in executive session to declare it illegal.

We believe the world now needs intelligent restoration of cannabis, especially for medical intervention.

> Rev. 22:14 *"Blessed are they that do his commandments, that they may have right to the tree of life, and may enter in through the gates into the city."*

MORMON SCRIPTURE DREAMING ABOUT GANJA: "The Tree of Life" "The River Of Water" "The Rod of Iron"

NEPHI, CHAPTER 8:

The following is quoted from the eighth chapter of the book of Nephi – in Mormon text.

> *"1. And it came to pass that we had gathered together all manner of seeds of every kind, and also of the seeds of fruit of every kind.*
>
> *2. And it came to pass that while my father tarried in the wilderness he spake unto us, saying, Behold, I have dreamed a dream; or, in other words, I have seen a vision...*
>
> *9. And it came to pass after I had prayed unto the Lord I beheld a large and spacious field.*
>
> *10. And it came to pass that I beheld a tree whose fruit was desirable to make one happy.*
>
> *11. And it came to pass that I did go forth and partake of the fruit thereof; and I beheld that it was most sweet, above all that I ever before tasted...*
>
> *12. And as I partook of the fruit thereof it filled my soul with exceeding great joy, wherefore, I began to be desirous that my family should partake of it also; for I knew that it was desirable above all other fruit.*

13. And as I cast my eyes round about, that perhaps I might discover my family also, I beheld a "river of water, and it ran along, and it was near the tree of which I was partaking the fruit.

24. And it came to pass that I beheld others pressing forward, and they came forth and caught hold of the end of the rod of iron; and they did press forward through the mist of darkness, clinging to the rod of iron, even until they did come forth and partake of the fruit of the tree.
25. And after they had partaken of the fruit of the tree they did cast their eyes about as if they were ashamed.

26. And I also cast my eyes round about, and beheld on the other side of the river of water a great and spacious building and it stood as it were in the sky high above the earth.

27. And it was filled with people, both old and young, both male and female; and their manner of dress was exceeding fine; and they were in the attitude of marking and pointing their fingers towards those who had come at and were partaking of the fruit...

33. And great was the multitude that did enter into that strange building. And after they did enter into that building they did point the finger of scorn at me and those that were partaking of the fruit also; but we heeded them not." *The parables are explained in the fifteenth chapter.*

1 NEPHI, CHAPTER 15:

"21. And it came to pass that they did speak unto me again, saying: What meaneth this thing which our father said in a dream? What meaneth the tree which he saw?

22. And I said unto them: It was a representation of the tree of life.

23. And they said unto me: What meaneth the rod of iron which our father saw, that led to the tree?

24. And I said unto them that it was the word of God; and whoso would hearken unto the word of God, and would hold fast unto it, they would never perish; neither could

the temptations and the fiery darts of the adversary overpower them unto blindness, to lead them away to destruction.

25. Wherefore, I, Nephi, did exhort them to give heed unto the word of the Lord; yea, I did exhort them with all the energies of my soul, and with all the faculty which I possessed, that they would give heed to the word of God and remember to keep his commandments always in all things.

26. And they said unto me: What meaneth the river of water which our father saw?

27. And I said unto them that it was an awful gulf, which separated the wicked from the tree of life and also from the saints of God...

34. But behold, I say unto you, the kingdom of God is not filthy, and there cannot any unclean thing enter into the kingdom of God; wherefore there must needs be a place of filthiness prepared for that which is filthy...

36. Wherefore, the wicked are rejected from the righteous, and also from that tree of life, whose fruit is most precious and most desirable above all other fruits; yea, and it is the greatest of all the gifts of God and thus I spake unto my brethren. Aman"

Ganja is the greatest of all the gifts of God!

CHAPTER 23
"REVELATIONS FROM MT. HOREB"

Over the centuries, there has been a great misunderstanding of the Bible passage found in Exodus 3, verses 1-2:

> "*[1]Now Moses kept his flock of Jethro, his father-in-law, the priest of Midian: and he led the flock to the backside of the desert, and came to the mountain of God, even to Horeb.*
>
> "*[2]And the angel of the Lord appeared unto him in a flame of fire, out of the midst of a BUSH and he looked and, behold, the BUSH was burned with FIRE and the BUSH was not consumed.*"

What was this bush? Different pagan religions, lacking understanding, have declared this "bush" to be a pine tree or a fir tree, and some burn it with fire to imitate this biblical passage. This is paganism. The only result of this is pine ash. But look what happened to Moses.

HE SAW GOD IN THE BUSH.

Exodus 3:3-4:

> "*[3]And Moses said, 'I will now turn aside and see this great sight, why the bush is not burnt.'*
>
> "*[4]And when the LORD saw that he turned aside to see, God called unto him in the midst of the BUSH and said 'Moses, Moses.' And he said 'Here am I.'*"

So it is obvious that Moses came to a higher understanding and consciousness in the BUSH, for he found himself reasoning with GOD HIMSELF. Pine ashes did not cause this. Could it be that this bush is actually the *plant of renown, the tree of wisdom, the tree of life* — The OLD GANJA BUSH?

We of the Coptic Church burn a natural BUSH in communion with our Brothers, passing our communion pipe, one to another. A sacrifice, made by fire unto God; its purpose in creation is a fiery sacrifice unto our God and Savior. Through this communion, we see God in our brother and God in ourselves.

We at the Coptic Church declare that what this passage refers to is the Sacramentality of Ganja which Moses partook of (this bush [GANJA]). Moses reasoned with his brother (the kingdom of God is within Man) on Mt. Horeb and saw God. Thus, he began to speak with God.

The Book of Joel, Chapter 2, verse 30 states:

> "And I will shew wonders in the heavens and in the earth; blood and fire, and pillars of smoke."

Book of Genesis, Chapter 15, verse 17:

> "And it came to pass, that, when the sun went down, and it was dark, behold a smoking furnace and a burning lamp that passes between those pieces."

The Book of Exodus, Chapter 20, verse 18:

> "And the people saw the thunderings, and the lightnings, and the noise of trumpet and the mountain [man is a mountain] smoking: and when the people saw it, they removed, stood afar off."

The Book of Isaiah, Chapter 42, verse 3:

> "A bruised reed will thou not break, and the smoking flax will be not quenched: he will bring forth judgment unto truth."

The Book of Matthew, Chapter 12, verse 20:

> "A bruised reed will he not break, and smoking flax will he not quench, till he send forth judgment unto victory."

The Book of Revelations, Chapter 1, verse 7:

> "Behold, he cometh with clouds [of smoke] and every eye will see him, and they also which pierced him, and they also which pierced him: and all kindreds of the earth will wail because of him. Even so, AMAN."

Psalms 18, verse 12:

"At the brightness that was before him his thick clouds passed, hail stones and coals of fire."

The Ethiopian Zion Coptic Church declares:

1. The Sacramentality of Ganja
2. The Pre-eminence of Judgment.
3. The Priesthood of Coptic.

The Holy Bible clearly states that the second coming of Christ will be "in the clouds" or "in the burning bush" as Moses saw God (so it was — so it is).

"Behold he cometh with clouds" and "thy truth reaches into the clouds."

The Ethiopian Zion Coptic Church is the Church that cometh with clouds. The story is the same, except you are there.

"Lo he comes, with clouds ascending."
"Once for favored sinners lives."
"Thousands, thousands, saints attending."
"Swells the triumph of Loves stream."
"Sweet perfume upon the breeze."
"Is born of ever vernal trees."
"And FLOWERS that never fading grow."
"Where streams of life forever flow."

You are there on Mt. Horeb.

CHAPTER 24
"The Sacramental Rights of Mankind"

By Walter Wells - elder priest EZCC

"Ganja is the sacramental right of all mankind, in today's sin-sick world. It is the Divine spirit of God among mankind, to unite us in the spirit of Love: to be one in this present time."

FROM THE FOUNDATION OF THE EARTH

In the beginning, the fruit of the tree in the midst of the garden was the fruit of Life and of knowledge of Good and Evil. It was partaken of by the Holy Angels (Holy Man) to preserve life and enable them to walk upright in the sight of their Creator: having the knowledge of good and evil.

By partaking of this fruit, they became wise and so were able to walk upon the earth without transgressing the commands of their King and Creator. They were able also to rule their households with integrity and prudence, keeping their wives and children in subjection. There was no divisive spirit among mankind, everyone being of one spirit, one language, and one speech.

It was a disastrous blow to the brotherhood of mankind when one holy brother, who was taught the difference between good and evil, became covetous and so fell from Grace. He was known as Satan, The Devil or Lucifer in plain words. He was the Deceiver of mankind: to entreat him from the natural things of creation to imaginations.

Satan was cast out from the holy brotherhood of mankind as an outcast upon the earth. He knows that the *Tree of Life* is partaken of in order to preserve life and to open man's knowledge to good and evil.

As time went by and man began to increase, God saw that corruption and violence were widespread among mankind; and their hearts were filled with evil imaginations, and so He vowed to destroy mankind for their wickedness. Only Noah, his sons, and his sons' wives were saved. A new covenant was established in Noah's sons: Shem, Ham, and Japheth, in whom all nations of the earth were thereafter divided. Shem was the father of the Hebrews, Japheth was the father of the Gentiles and Ham was the father of the Canaanites, who later proclaimed a false god in Nimrod, that mighty hunter.

Because of evil imaginations, mankind forgot the principles of the HOLY BROTHERHOOD and started to make images of stone and wood; and to worship them. As a result, the nations of the earth were scattered abroad on the face of the earth; their languages confounded so that they could not unite. As time passed and the hearts of men grew desperately wicked, God found pleasure and great faith in Abraham, the Hebrew, who walked upright in the laws and precepts of his Creator, and this was counted as righteousness.

God, therefore, made a covenant with him and promised that the forthcoming Savior of the entire human race would spring from his seed. Under the reign of the Messiah, the sacrifice of goats and bulls which were required as a Sacrifice of Atonement according to the Laws and Covenants between God and Man would be changed, and the fiery Sacrifice of Incense from the chalice would be required for the Purification of Sins. (Not something new, yet new to this world. For Angels [the sanctified of mankind] have always kept the way of the Tree of Life.)

In other words, every man is responsible, individually, for his sins and as such is required to prepare his body: Holy and acceptable to God. This body could only be made pure by confessing and putting away the deeds of the flesh and attaining to the Spirit, which giveth Life.

The **Herb is the Sacrifice** for the purification of the human heart and **for the preservation of life eternally**. It is the Sacrifice representing the body and blood of Christ, which he offered as a sacrifice for the entire human race. A sacrifice wherein, as often as we partake thereof, we would ever be put in remembrance of our Brother, Christ; who, because of his great Love for all mankind, laid down his life for us, his friends. Indeed, we can truly say "No greater Love hath any man than this."

Christ did this because he knew that the entire human race was one divine brotherhood of which he was a part. His mission was for the unification of humanity as one people; even as we were in the early days before the rise of the false god, Nimrod.

Through the disobedience of God's chosen people and their failure to unite, the doors of Salvation were closed to all mankind, except those who were willing to turn from their wickedness and do the lawful things of God.

As a result: the Sacrifice of Purification (Ganja) through the Grace of God to Man.

History will recall that during Moses' leadership of Israel: they were gathered together before the mountain (Man) to hear the commandments of the Lord to his people. While they gathered, they observed Holy Man partaking of the Holy sacrifice which was consumed by fire. While there, they were spoken to by Moses, who was partaking of the Holy Incense, in order to gain wisdom and understanding to teach his people in such a time of great peril.

Moses told Israel that they should always remember what they saw during their gathering, and should not bow to imaginations as the days passed on. "For" said he, "God spoke to you out of the fire, yet ye heard not." He warned against the corruption of self in the making of images or even to worship the physical sun and moon and stars.

Our God is man (the consuming fire). When we fail to offer sacrifice and praise to Man, we would be cut off as charged by God in his covenant with mankind. We would be scattered among the nations of the earth, and would be left few in numbers. We would also be tempted into worshipping gods made by men's hands; wood and stone which neither hear nor eat nor smell.

John, who was baptizing the Jews according to the laws of Moses, prophesied of the fiery baptism wherein all mankind would partake, both Jews and Gentiles. The baptism of John could only lead to repentance; however, the fiery baptism of Christ led to eternal life.

St. John the Divine was called to witness the future of mankind on earth, at which time, he prophesied of these present times when HERB would be the unquestionable sacrifice offered for the redemption of Man's sinful nature. He saw the Angels of God with their golden censer or pipe; with much Incense (Ganja) to offer prayers upon the Altar (Man). It has been said that the smoke of the incense ascended to God.

Today it is the same pipe and Herb that man is required to partake of for the cleansing of the soul. The Prophet John witnessed the happenings of this present generation—according to Biblical prophecy. He envisioned the final purification of mankind.

This was possible through Man's participation of the *Tree of Life*, which is known today as Ganja. This tree is for the healing of the nations.

There would be no more curse; blessings would now flow as the generations return to worship the true and living God: "Man." In these times we will become conscious as to who God really is, seeing that His name is written in our forehead. We are accorded rights to the *Tree of Life*; as long as we walk in the commandments and precepts of God. Whosoever will accept Christ will freely partake of his Sacrament: Ganja.

> Rev. 22:2 – *"In the midst of the street of it, and on either side of the river, was there the tree of life, which bare twelve manner of fruits, and yielded her fruit every month: and the leaves of the tree were for the healing of the nation."*

> Rev. 22:14 – *"Blessed are they that do his commandments, that they may have right to the tree of life, and may enter in through the gates into the city."*

To the generation of today's world I say:

> Deut. 5:3-4 – *"³Our Lord made not this covenant with our fathers, but with us, even us, who are all of us here alive this day. ⁴The Lord talked with you face to face in the mount out of the midst of the fire."*

> Isa. 59:1 – *"Behold the Lord's hand is not shortened, that it cannot save; neither his ear heavy that it cannot hear."*

God is not far from us, neither is he hidden from us.

He is not in the sky that one should say, "Who will go up and bring him down so we can hear him?" Neither is he beyond the sea that one should say, "Who is going to cross the sea to bring him to us?" Yet the word is nigh to us, even in our mouths and hearts, that we will keep them. Today, even in our tribulations, our God will wash away the filth of the daughters of Zion, and purge our blood with the spirit of Judgment and the spirit of burning (Ganja). He will create upon every man a cloud and smoke by day; and the shining of a flaming fire by night.

> Isaiah 4: 4-5 – *"⁴When the Lord shall have washed away the filth of the daughters of Zion, and shall have purged*

the blood of Jerusalem from the midst there of by the spirit of judgment, and by the spirit of burning. ⁵And the Lord will create upon every dwelling place of mount Zion, and upon her assemblies, a cloud and smoke by day, and the shining of a flaming fire by night: for upon all the glory shall be a defense."

Men have been separated from God because of their iniquities. Their hands are defiled with blood, their lips have spoken lies and their tongue perverseness. None calleth for Justice nor pleadeth for Truth. They trust in vanity; they conceive mischief and bring forth iniquity.

The ETHIOPIAN ZION COPTIC CHURCH: will not hold its peace; until the Righteousness thereof goes forth as brightness and Salvation as a lamp that burneth. The Gentiles will see our righteousness, and all kings our glory, and we will be called by our "NEW NAME – RASTAFARI - THE ALMIGHTY." For we are Crown of Glory in the hand of the Lord; and a ROYAL DIADEM, in the hands of our God. We will be called: "THE HOLY PEOPLE"; "THE REDEEMED OF THE LORD"; "SOUGHT OUT" and "A CITY NOT FORSAKEN." (Isaiah 62: 12)

The entire brotherhood of mankind, worldwide; I ask that each one will open their understanding to the TRUTH OF THE DOCTRINE: as handed down from our fathers. We of the Coptic Faith, cannot depart therefrom; as we have made a covenant with our God, to keep HIS COMMANDMENTS and to WALK UPRIGHT in his sight. Because we have walked in these precepts, we of the Coptic Church, being the advocate of the fulfillment of these prophesies can today truly say:

"SPIRIT OF THE LORD GOD RASTAFARI IS UPON US; BECAUSE HE HATH ANOINTED US TO PREACH GOOD TIDINGS UNTO THE MEEK: HE HATH SENT US TO BIND UP THE BROKENHEARTED, TO PROCLAIM LIBERTY TO THE CAPTIVES, AND THE OPENING OF THE PRISON TO THEM THAT ARE BOUND; TO PROCLAIM ACCEPTABLE MAN OF THE LORD, AND THE DAY OF VENGEANCE OF OUR GOD: TO COMFORT ALL THAT MOURN. TO APPOINT UNTO THEM THAT MOURN ZION, TO GIVE UNTO THEM BEAUTY FOR ASHES, THE OIL OF JOY FOR MOURNING, THE GARMENT OF PRAISE FOR THE SPIRIT OF HEAVINESS; THEY TOO WILL BE CALLED A FORTRESS OF RIGHTEOUSNESS, THE PLANTING OF THE LORD, THAT HE WILL BE GLORIFIED. AND WE WILL BUILD THE

OLD WASTES AND RAISE UP THE FORMER DESOLATIONS, AND WE WILL REPAIR THE WASTE CITIES: THE DESOLATION OF MANY GENERATIONS.

"YET WE WILL BE NAMED THE PRIESTS OF THE LORD: MEN WILL CALL US THE MINISTERS OF OUR GOD.

"EVERLIVING JOY WILL BE UNTO US. FOR OUR LORD GOD LOVETH JUDGMENT. HE HATH DIRECTED OUR WORK IN TRUTH: AND HATH MADE AN EVERLIVING COVENANT WITH US. OUR SEED WILL BE KNOWN AMONG THE GENTILES, OUR OFFSPRING AMONG THE PEOPLE. ALL THAT SEE US WILL ACKNOWLEDGE US; THAT WE ARE THE SEED WHICH THE LORD HATH BLESSED. WE WILL GREATLY REJOICE IN THE LORD, AND OUR SOUL WILL BE JOYFUL IN OUR GOD; FOR HE HATH CLOTHED US WITH THE GARMENTS OF SALVATION: HE HATH COVERED US WITH THE ROBE OF RIGHTEOUSNESS, AS A BRIDEGROOM DECKETH HIMSELF WITH ORNAMENTS, AND AS A BRIDE ADORNETH HERSELF WITH HER JEWELS. FOR AS THE EARTH BRINGETH FORTH HER BUD, AND AS THE GARDEN CAUSETH THINGS THAT ARE SOWN IN IT TO SPRING FORTH; SO THE LORD GOD RASTAFARI HAS CAUSED HIS RIGHTEOUSNESS AND PRAISE TO SPRING FORTH BEFORE ALL THE NATIONS. SELAH."

Signed Walter E. Wells

Spiritual Leader—Coptic Church

CHAPTER 25
"MARIJUANA AS THE ONLY PEACEMAKER IN THIS GENERATION"

Marijuana is the only peacemaker in this generation; marijuana can help one to know himself and his relationship to God as a son or heir.

The scripture says, "mark the perfect man and behold the upright, for the end of that man is peace." To be at peace with oneself is the greatest fulfillment that one can find. And from the time you can make peace with yourself, you make peace with others.

Love is the pre-requisite for peace. Love is defined in the scripture as the keeping of the commandments: For if you love me you won't steal from me, or covet me, or bare false witness against me; or commit adultery with my spouse; or do any other thing that would harm me or my loved ones. To know love is to know God; for God is love. To know God, mankind has to embrace every Godly attribute... such as morality, patience, perseverance, faith, hope, charity, longsuffering, mercy, joy (the scripture refers to these as fruits of the spirit) and even anger or righteous indignation.

- For God is angry with the wicked every day, especially the conscious wicked - the ones who make conscious decisions, knowing that those decisions are going to lead to human suffering. Like the decisions to fight against those who would use the "Biblical Tree of Life."

Rev. 21:3 – *"And I heard a great voice out of heaven saying, Behold, the tabernacle of God is with man, and he will dwell with them, they shall be his people, and God himself shall be with them, be their God."*

God has no place in his kingdom for corruption. Therefore, this corruption must put on incorruption and this mortal must put on immortality. And this is Life Eternal that we will know Thee, the only true God and *Jes-us Christus* whom thou hast sent.

Marijuana is a communion between all races. Furthermore, marijuana is able to heal the spiritual separation now experienced by all Peoples; by uniting ALL Peoples with One Free and uncorrupted spirit contained within the natural herb —marijuana.

Marijuana is a sacrifice of Peace wherein mankind will study war no more, covet no more, hate no more; yet in one accord we will join hearts and hands together, giving praise to God Almighty; who doeth all things well.

CHAPTER 26
"MARIJUANA AS A MEDICINE"

Beit Shemesh, near Jerusalem, has documented cannabis medicine in the area around the time of the formation of the Roman Catholic Church. It was used as an aid in *childbearing*.

Study: Marijuana was used in childbirth

New York, N.Y. (AP.) — Ashes from a fourth-century tomb near Jerusalem suggest that marijuana plants may have been used in the ancient Middle East to help childbirth, claim researchers.

The tomb contained the remains of a teenager who apparently died while giving or during the last stages of pregnancy.

Analysis indicated that ashes found with the skeleton came from cannabis, the marijuana plant. Apparently, cannabis was burned for use as an inhalant to aid childbirth, expressed researchers; noting that a 19th-century medical publication shows it strengthened contractions while reducing labor pain.

Medicinal use of cannabis was recorded in Egypt in the 16th century B.C., the Israeli scientists said in today's issue of the journal *Nature*.

The Des Moines Register, May 20, 1993, page 9A.

HEMP FOR HEALTH

"Medical uses of Hemp include treating back pain, asthma, glaucoma, epilepsy, cancer, muscle spasms, migraines tumors, Stress, depression and anorexia.

"It is an antibiotic and expectorant, useful in muscle ointments and to treat arthritis and rheumatism. Hundreds of other therapeutic uses are likely, but hard-to-get permits are required to use it, and the federal government banned research into medical use of Hemp, so millions of people continue to suffer needlessly, and a valuable herbal medicine with minimal side-effects is held hostage by out-of-date laws."

"Cannabis users statistically live one or two years longer than non-users. Hemp offers affordable health care for America."

MORE RESEARCH IS NEEDED - "At the 1975 National Institute of Drug Abuse (NIDA) Asilomar Conference, participants were amazed at the documented results of marijuana research and agreed that a massive national research project was in order. Instead, all federal research grants were terminated in 1976 and subsequent private research been heavily restricted."

CHAPTER 27
"MARIJUANA AS FOOD"

Hemp seed was used in porridge, soups, and gruel by virtually all people of the world, daily, until this century.

Monks were required to eat it three times a day, make their clothes from hemp, and print their bibles on hemp. (Therapeutic Potential of Marijuana and "Research Institute for Study of Mars," and Eastern Orthodox Church)

WHY AS FOOD?

The Marijuana (Hemp) seed (which is technically a fruit) is the second most complete vegetable protein source on our planet; number one is soybeans.

Australia survived two prolonged famines in the 19th Century using virtually nothing but marijuana seed for protein and its leaves for roughage. (Australian history books and The Marijuana Farmers by Jack Frazier, 1972)

Pot seed is the highest in enzymes and amino acids of any food on our planet (including soybeans), and can be made (like soybeans) to taste like chicken, steak, pork, tofu, margarine, etc. at 5% to 10% the cost of soybean protein, (you could also feed all domesticated animals for less than 20% of current cost.) [Therapeutic Potential of Mari.; The Marijuana Farmer].

Hemp seed is the single healthiest food on the planet and can grow on land that cannot grow anything else profitably. Also, hemp is one of the world's best rotation crops (re-nitrogenates the soil). (U.S. Dept. of Agriculture)

With government cooperation, in two to five years, the Marijuana seed (alone) would be instrumental in finally wiping out this silly world starvation caused by protein hunger.

SUMMARY

Due to the prosecution of God's church from the beginning of the Christian era, and, due to the persecution against marijuana, the true understanding of the Eucharist has remained hidden from Christendom and the world, only to be revealed in these times – the culmination of all human history.

We of the Ethiopian Zion Coptic Church declare marijuana for the communion of saints, forgiveness of sins, and for the resurrection of mankind. The fruits of the mystery are remembrance of the passions and death of Christ, propitiation for sins, defense against temptations and the indwelling of Christ in the faithful.

Preparations for communion consist of confession of sins, fasting from sin, and reconciliation with all mankind. As such, the participant in the Eucharist will be in a condition in which prayer and meditation are easy and fruitful. He will find his emotion purified and stimulated, his spirituality quickened and his heart filled with love.

CHAPTER 28
"WHY THE CONTINUING OPPRESSION?"

The use of Marijuana has been shown again and again to be a rather benign practice. Below is some recent history relating to Marijuana.

The Encyclopedia of Psychoactive Drugs- Marijuana- by Solomon Snyder:

1840-1900 - Over 100 articles appear in medical journals in which marijuana is recommended for various medical purposes.

1870 - Marijuana is listed in the U.S. Pharmacopeia as for various illnesses.

1895 - The English Indian Hemp Drug Commission states that moderate use of marijuana has no evil.

1922-1925 - U.S. troops are smoking marijuana in Panama: the Panama Canal Zone Report concludes that there is no evidence that marijuana usage is habit forming or deleterious; the report recommends that no action be taken to prevent the use or sale of marijuana.

1943 - The editor of the journal Military Surgeon states that although some military personnel smoke marijuana, he does not view it as a problem.

1943 - The La Guardia report states that the medical, psychological, and social problems attributed to marijuana usage have been exaggerated.

1972 - The National Commission of Marijuana and Drug Abuse, appointed by President Nixon and headed by Raymond Schaefer, the former governor of Pennsylvania, recommends the decriminalization of marijuana.

1975-1976 - "Results support the apparent conclusion that in terms of intellectual functions such as cognition, motivation, memory, and in terms of perceptual-motor skills such as motor coordination, sustained attention, and reaction time, long term use of marijuana produces insignificant effects."

—Hall, F.B.; Klein, AL; and Walters, J.E. long term effects of marijuana smoking. Journal of Altered States of Consciousness, 2(2):161-170, 1975-1976)

1979 - "Users of marijuana differ from nonusers on a cluster of attributes reflecting unconventionality, nontraditionality or nonconformity. Users tend to be more open to experience; more esthetically oriented; and more interested in creativity, play novelty or spontaneity than nonusers" —Jessor, R., Marijuana: a review of recent psychosocial research. Handbook on Drug Abuse. NIDA, 1979. Pg. 337- 355.

1980 - "Smokers, nonsmokers, and former smokers did not differ from each other in term of social or emotional adjustment, alienation, aggression, or reactions to frustrations."
—Pascale, R; Hurd, M.; Primavera, L.H. Journal of Social Psychology, 110:273-283, 1980.

1980 - "Heavy marijuana use was often correlated with employment stability, low unemployment, and acquisition of material goods."

—Carter, W.E. ed. Cannabis in Costa Rica: A Study of Chronic Marijuana Use. Philadelphia, PA. Institute for the Study of Human Issues, 1980.

1982 - The National Task Force on Cannabis Regulation issues a report in which it proposes alternatives to the current policy of marijuana prohibition.

The National Academy of Sciences recommends the decriminalization of marijuana. It stated that there is "no conclusive evidence that marijuana causes permanent, long-term health damage in humans...or causes birth defects."

1990 - "This is a remarkable statement. First, the record on marijuana encompasses five thousand years of human experience. Second, marijuana is now used daily by an enormous number of people throughout the world. Estimates suggest that from 20 million to 50 million Americans routinely, albeit illegally, smoke marijuana without the benefit of direct medical supervision. Yet despite this long history of use and the extraordinarily high number of social smokers, there are simply no medical reports to suggest that consuming marijuana has caused a single death." **He also said marijuana is one of the safest therapeutic substances known to man.** —**US Department of Justice, Drug Enforcement Administration; Docket No. 86-22; Francis Young, Administrative Law Judge.**

New York Times, May3, 1991, pg. 11A. - *Cancer Specialists Favor Marijuana As Medicine* – "Nearly half of the cancer specialists responding to a questionnaire on the controversial subject of marijuana used as medicine said they would prescribe the drug if it were legal, researchers at Harvard University said. A slightly smaller percentage of the specialists answering the mailed questionnaire said that despite the illegality of the drug, they had already recommended it to patients as a way of finding relief from nausea resulting from chemotherapy and for enhancing appetite."

Ann Landers - In her column of May 21, 1991, she states, "I have long supported the use of marijuana for medicinal purposes. It has indeed proven helpful to asthmatics, as well as cancer and glaucoma patients. Marijuana can and should be made available for these purposes."

A recent survey of members of the Association for Clinical Oncology, printed in the July 1991 issue of Journal of Clinical Oncology, found that 44% of the respondents recommended marijuana to their patients in spite of marijuana's illegality, and 73% of those with opinions considered marijuana to be both safe and effective.

Late 1992: German court declares drug laws invalid —

Berlin – Declaring Germany's laws against drug use unconstitutional because they infringe on the "free development of personality," an appellate court said Germans have the same right to alter their mental State on cannabis as they do by using liquor or cigarettes.

The court in Luebeck, in Northern Germany, threw out a conviction in a case involving a woman found with 4 one-hundredths of an ounce of hashish in her sock. Judge Wolfgang Neskovic said German law requires the state to treat cannabis-based drugs just as it does alcohol and tobacco because "alcohol and tobacco (are) considerably more damaging than hashish."

Support for marijuana legalization comes not only from those concerned about the erosion of civil liberties, but from some of North America's most eminent scholars, medical experts and experts in almost every professional field, as well as, top officials and experts in the judicial, legal, and political areas. Ten states have decriminalized up to an ounce and up until quite recently; one could grow a couple of plants for personal use in Alaska. The federal government is very reluctantly supplying government-grown marijuana to glaucoma and cancer patients, even though 33 States have enacted legislation realizing that marijuana has medical uses. The argument that marijuana poses serious health risks and has no accepted safe use are highly suspect, to say the least.

David Friedman, Deputy Director of the National Institute on Drug Abuse's preclinical research division and the official in charge of overseeing the agency's marijuana research said, "But in terms of a direct physical threat to the body, it's probably true that [marijuana's] greatest danger is if a bale of it falls on you." Washington post, Sept. 19, 1990, at A 19.

A California state advisory commission, which was created by the Legislature in 1969 and appointed by state agencies and the governor, recently recommended that California legalizes marijuana. Los Angeles Times, August 18, 1990, at 35, col. 1.

All this evidence indicates that marijuana is not the evil that the United Nations and the Congress of the U.S. have labeled it to be. What evil are they speaking about? Is it because users tend to question authority, to be unconventional, non-traditional, or nonconformist. Remember, it was the Roman Empire that labeled Christians as such and persecuted them to the ends of the earth.

Today the United Nations and the U.S. Government both have declared international war against those who would use marijuana. By doing so, both are in disagreement with those sacred documents that they purport to live by.

The U.N. Universal Declaration of Human Rights, Article 4, declares that participation in the cultural life of the community is a right. The Charter of the United Nations, Chapter I Article 1 (1) respects "the principle of equal rights and self-determination of peoples..." Article 1 (3) promotes the "fundamental freedoms for all without distinction as to race, sex, language or religion."

Each of the first ten Amendments of the Bill of Rights, with the exception of the third, is desecrated by the marijuana laws. The acts substantially impose infamous punishments, banishments, disenfranchisements, disqualifications, near loss of citizenship, and forfeiture of property upon members of a group of persons embracing a particular philosophy and/or ideology and/or acting a certain way to the displeasure of Congress, or the medical community.

The United Nations and the political governments who assist in this conspiracy are in violation of basic God-given human rights. Rights extending in history from the Bible, through the Magna Carta, to their enumeration in the Bill of Rights of the Constitution of the United States of America ("the Supreme law of the land" Article VI:2).

The official attacks that deny humanity their religious rights and cultural visions are horrible. The seizure of property and assets, the revocation and denial of professional licenses, the kidnapping of children from their homes, urine testing, imprisonment, and/or the forcible indoctrination (treatment) of marijuana users are all tactics meant (in the words of The Genocide Convention Implementation Act of 1987) to "destroy in whole or substantial part." History records that NAZI doctors and their preoccupation with "mental hygiene" were a driving force in the Holocaust.

In 1989, the U.S. surpassed South Africa and remains the world's leading prison state to this day. There was a big outcry in 1979 when former UN Ambassador Andrew Young told the world that the U.S. had more political prisoners than any other nation. (Amnesty International 3 ACLU)

The essence of the ideology is its capacity to hide control behind the magic cloak of therapeutic help. Thus, medicine is the paradigm for modernized domination. Indeed, its cultural hegemony is so potent that the very meaning of politics is being re-defined. Politics is (usually) interactive – the debate of citizens regarding purpose, value, and power. Medicalized politics is unilateral - the decision of the "helpers" on behalf of the "helped."

Taken from *The Emperor Wears No Clothes*:

"'Thomas Jefferson's immortal words, "*I have sworn upon the altar of God eternal hostility against every form of tyranny over the mind of man" are engraved into the marble of his memorial in Washington D.C.'"*

Historians indicate that for the first 300 to 400 years A.D., Christian sects were gentle and loving, open, tolerant and unstructured: a poor man's or slave's religion. This was until Roman Emperor Constantine feigned conversion to Christianity and set up the Roman Catholic Church. This became the official religion of the empire and anyone who didn't agree was persecuted.

In a series of councils, all contrary dogmas were outlawed and driven underground during the Dark Ages 400-900 A.D. All European people were forced to adhere to the "*Holy*" Roman Empire's policy, with blind faith, in one unquestioned version of how to worship God... and the Pope's infallibility. Political rulers and merchants aided and abetted this fraud.

During this time, the people were forbidden to learn to read or write and often were punished or put to death for doing so.

While embracing wine as a sacrament, the Inquisition outlawed cannabis ingestion in Spain in the 12th century and France in the 13th century. Anyone using hemp to communicate, heal, or otherwise was labeled "Witch." In 1484, Pope Innocent VIII proclaimed hemp an unholy sacrament of the second and third types of satanic mass, which lasted more than 150 years.

Taken from *Time*, Aug. 21, 1989, Article "Do Humans Need to Get High?":

Dr. Lester Grinspoon, a Harvard psychiatrist and author of several books on drugs, states:

"I have come to the view that humans have a need - perhaps even a drive - to alter their state of consciousness from time to time." Pioneer drug researcher Dr. Andrew Weil of the University of Arizona College of Medicine confirms that view: *"There is not a shred of hope from history or from cross-cultural studies to suggest that human beings can live without substances."*

Ronald K. Siegel, a consultant on the nature of drug addiction to two presidential commissions, the National Institute on Drug Abuse and the World Health Organization, in his book "In Intoxication: Life in Pursuit of Artificial Paradise," concluded that the desire to alter one's state of consciousness is a drive as elemental as hunger, thirst, and sex.

Siegel argues that the war on drugs is doomed because it is against man's own nature. His controversial contention: humanity's pursuit of happiness through substances is a universal and inescapable fact of life.

In a truly free and democratic society, how can one justify the war against marijuana and those who choose to use it. A lot of very intelligent and influential people have smoked marijuana and some continue to use it. All indications are that the Founding Fathers of the United States used marijuana. Note the following article from The Tribal Messenger:

POT AND PRESIDENTS

Marijuana smoking is quite popular in the U.S. today, but few people realize that pot was once so popular in the Country—that 7 U.S. presidents used it.

Dr. Burke, President of the American Historical Reference Society and consultant for the Smithsonian Institute, included the following U.S. Presidents as marijuana users: George Washington, Thomas Jefferson, James Madison, James Monroe, Andrew Jackson, Zachary Taylor, and Franklin Pierce.

Pot was common among tobacco growers, for when it was mixed with tobacco, it gave a mild intoxicating effect. The leaves and resins (hashish) were used to season food and as a medicine.

Prior to the Civil War, pot was a very successful drug when used to cure insomnia and impotence. It was used primarily to reduce tension.

"Early letters from our founding fathers often refer to the pleasures of hemp smoking," said Dr. Burke. There are even references to it in the Congressional Record. Marijuana never became a commercial industry because the plant was too easy to grow.

George Washington, James Madison, and Thomas Jefferson all cultivated pot on their plantations. George Washington is said to have preferred a good pipeful of "the leaves of hemp" to any alcoholic drink.

Thomas Jefferson and George Washington often corresponded about the virtues of smoking hemp and are said to have traded parcels of it as gestures of friendship.

James Madison once remarked that had it not been for hemp, he would not have had the insights he had in the work of creating a new and democratic nation.

James Monroe, the creator of the Monroe Doctrine, smoked both pot and hashish. Madison brought back the habit of smoking hashish from France and continued smoking until he was 73.

Pierce, Taylor and Jackson, all military men, smoked pot with their troops. As popular as pot smoking is today in Vietnam, it was twice as popular among our soldiers in the Mexican War. Pierce wrote home to his family that it was about the only thing good about the war.

---The Tribal Messenger

15 PEOPLE WHO HAVE TAKEN HASHISH OR MARIJUANA:

Book of Lists:

1. Pythagoras (d. c. 497 B.C.), Greek philosopher, mathematician, and religious reformer.
2. Victor Hugo (1802-1885), French writer.
3. Theophile Gautier (1811-1885), French writer and critic.
4. Charles Baudelaire (1821-1867), French poet.
5. Fitz Hugh Ludlow (1836-1870), U.S. journalist.
6. Stephane Mallarme (1842-1898), French poet.
7. Friedrich Nietzsche (1844-1900), German philosopher.
8. Alice B. Toklas (1877-1967), U.S. great and good friend of Gertrude Stein.
9. Guillaume Apollinaire (1880-1918), French writer
10. Diego Rivera (1886-1957), Mexican painter.
11. MezzMezzrow (1899-1959), U.S. jazz musician.
12. Errol Flynn (1909-1973), U.S. actor.
13. Gene Krupa (1909-1973), U.S musician.
14. John F. Kennedy (1917-1963), U.S. president.
15. Robert Mitchum (b. 1917), U.S. actor.

Abraham Lincoln 1840:

"Prohibition... goes beyond the bounds of reason, in that it attempts to control a man's appetite by legislation and makes a crime out of things that are not crimes... A prohibition law strikes a blow at the very principles upon which our government was founded."

President Jimmy Carter addressed Congress Aug. 2, 1977, saying: "Penalties against possession of a drug should not be more damaging to an individual than the use of the drug itself. Therefore, I support legislation amending federal law to eliminate all federal criminal penalties for the possession of up to one ounce of marijuana."

Recently elected President Bill Clinton admitted to trying marijuana during his presidential campaign and told the people he didn't inhale.

Is ganja smoking really harmful? By Ronald G. Lampart:

"In the Gleaner of Monday, January 28, is a report on the Caribbean Child Development Centre Workshop, in Kingston. At this workshop, a study showed that there was no significant difference between babies born to ganja-smoking mothers and those born to non-smoking mothers during pregnancy, at birth, or for the six subsequent years these infants were followed up.

"Among the researchers were a developmental psychologist, two consultants in infant behaviour, an ethnographer, 14 research assistants, including three nurses who were attached to the Princess Margaret Hospital, where all the babies were delivered.

"The total cost of the study was $655,000 US (J$5.2 million) all of which came from the U.S.A. and helped with our foreign exchange.

"This study was unique for its comprehensiveness and control. As only marijuana was involved; none of the mothers smoked tobacco and none had anything to do with crack or cocaine — those two dangerous and highly addictive substances which our leaders have introduced into this country by their relentless overseas-motivated war on ganja. Incidentally, this is a claim also made by

the authorities in Belize, where the problem of crack and cocaine has reached an almost uncontrollable situation.

"It may be interesting to note that of the 59 infants followed up, the six-year-old with the highest intelligence rating is from the smoking mothers' group.

"But this article is not about this study, nor is it about the detailed one done by the UWI in 1972. That whole report, with its conclusions, was published in 46 consecutive editions of the Gleaner from June 3 to August 8, 1972. But the findings, it seems, were ignored by our leaders."

Does ganja cause madness? Dr. Freddie Hickling, a specialist in madness, says this is total rubbish (Gleaner, February 3, 1991):

"The U.S.A. is now the world's largest consumer of this product. There, it ranks second to corn as the largest agricultural cash crop, above wheat, barley and soya — a 16 billion dollar industry. (See Democracy Today, June 1989) She is also second to Mexico as the world's largest producer.

"Many times I see helicopters come over my area and spray ganja fields, and kill off other crops and even cattle in the process. When I know that this act is aided and sponsored by the World's second largest grower and its greatest consumer, I say to myself, 'This is madness. This cannot be justice.'

"Then I read of the draconian laws which make criminals of people and the massive fines on airlines and ships; when I know that the intent of the law has nothing to do with any dangers of the product, nor to the society, but merely to prevent its entry into the world's second largest producer and its greatest consumer: I say to myself 'Crazy' — this certainly cannot be justice. So I look up the records and I find that the American Bar Association, the American Medical Association, the American National Advisory Council on Criminal Justice, Standards and Goals, and the American National Council of Churches and others have gone on record in support of the removal of all criminal penalties for the private possession and use of marijuana.

"It is not surprising therefore that it is legal in Alaska and some other states. In the others, its possession or use is not a criminal offense and penalties for violation are in the same category as traffic fines."

H.P. Blavatsky, author of "The Secret Doctrine" and "Isis Unveiled," as well as the founder of the Theosophical Society, used the sacred Ganja for Devine insights and inspiration. She told lifelong friend A.L. Rawson, after 25 years of hashish use, "It is a wonderful drug and it clears up profound mysteries."

"A day will come when you will walk hand in hand, Pagans and Christians, with your eyes open, nourished with the Herb of Life.

"Fantasies will appear to you as fantasies, and you will stretch out your hands, so that of all that is vital, you too might hold something..."

~ Palamas ~

THE EMPEROR WEARS NO CLOTHES:

The following information came *from The Emperor No Clothes*, which is a very informative book about Hemp and The Marijuana Conspiracy. I strongly recommend that you read this historical account.

Marijuana and Hashish extracts were the second or third most prescribed medicines in the U.S. from 1842 until the 1890s. Its legal medicinal use continued until the Marijuana Tax Act of 1937.

When mechanical hemp fiber stripping machines were created in the mid-1930s, virtually all timber, paper, and large newspaper holding companies stood to lose billions and perhaps go bankrupt. Among the companies were Hearst Paper Manufacturing Division, Kimberly Clark (U.S.A) and St. Regis.

The late 1920s and 1930s saw continuing consolidation of power into the hands of a few large steel, oil, and chemical (munitions) companies. The U.S. federal government placed much of the textile production for the domestic economy in the hands of their chief munitions maker, DuPont.

DuPont had just patented processes to make plastic from oil and coal as well as new sulfite processes to make paper from wood pulp in1937. If hemp had not been made illegal, 80% of DuPont's business would never have come to be, nor would great majority of the population inflicted on U.S. Northwestern and Southeastern Rivers.

In the 1920s and 30s, the Hearst's newspaper chain led a deliberate yellow journalism campaign to have hemp outlawed. During the 1898 Spanish-American War, the Hearst's chain had 800,000 acres of its prime Mexican timberland seized by the marijuana smoking army of Pancho Villa. Shortly after this, the Hearst newspaper denounced Spaniards, Mexican-Americans, and Latinos. In the 1930s, the Hearst newspaper claimed it was marijuana-crazed Negros who were raping white women.

During this period of American history, brutal segregation laws were in effect; up until the 1950s and 60s. Hundreds of thousands of Mexicans and Negroes spent, in aggregate, millions of years in prisons; on chain gangs, for such crimes as stepping on white men's shadows, looking white people directly in the eye for 3 seconds or more, looking at a white woman twice, smoking marijuana, etc.

Testimony before Congress in 1937, for the purpose of outlawing hemp, consisted almost entirely of Hearst's and other sensational and racist newspaper articles, read aloud by Harry J. Anslinger, Director of the Federal Bureau of Narcotics (FBN) (This agency has since evolved into the Drug Enforcement Administration D.E.A.)

Prior to 1931, Anslinger was Assistant U.S. Commissioner for Prohibition. Anslinger was hand-picked by his uncle-in-law, Andrew Mellon, Secretary of the Treasury under President Herbert Hoover. The same Andrew Mellon was the owner of the sixth largest bank (in 1937) in the U.S., the Mellon Bank in Pittsburgh, one of only two bankers for DuPont from 1928 to the present.

In 1937, Anslinger testified before Congress, saying Marijuana is the most violence-causing drug in the history of mankind.

In fact, F.B.I. statistics, had Anslinger bothered to check, showed at least 65% to 75% of all murders in the U.S. were then — and still are — alcohol related.

Between 1948 and 1950, Anslinger stopped feeding the press the story that marijuana was violence-causing and began Red Baiting, typical of the McCarthy era.

Now the frightened American public was told that this was a much more dangerous drug than originally thought. Testifying before a strongly anti-Communist Congress in 1948, Anslinger proclaimed that marijuana caused its users to become so peaceful and pacifistic! – that the Communists could and would use marijuana to weaken our American fighting men's will to fight.

From that time to this time many, many lies have been told about marijuana.

MORE ARE INDICATED IN THE CONSPIRACY:

According to NORMAL (The National Organization for the Reform of Marijuana Laws), High Times magazine and Omni magazine (September 1982) — Eli Lilly Co.; Abbott Labs; Pfizer; Smith; Kline and French; and others would lose hundreds of millions to billions of dollars annually if marijuana were legal in the U.S., and lose even more billions in the Third World.

The drug companies, at their own insistence, specifically by lobbying, got the Federal Government to prevent all positive research into medical marijuana in 1976, the last year of the Ford Administration.

Isn't it of curiosity that American drug companies and pharmacist groups supply almost half the funding for the 4000 Families Against Marijuana type organizations in America. The other half is supplied by Action, a federal VISTA agency, and by liquor and beer makers like Anheuser-Busch, Coors, Philip Morris, etc., or by the ad agencies who represent them (as public service). (Some 500,000 people are poisoned each year in Third World countries by drugs, pesticides, etc., that are sold to them by American companies which are banned from sale in U.S.)

ALSO FROM THE EMPEROR BOOK:

Hemp seed contains 30% (by volume) oil. This oil makes high-grade diesel fuel oil and aircraft engine and precision machine oil. Remember, throughout history hemp seed was made into fuel oil: the Genie's lamp burned hemp seed oil, as did Abraham, the prophets, and Abraham Lincoln.

Botanically, hemp is a member of the most advanced plant family on Earth. It is a dioeciously (i.e., having male, female and sometimes hermaphroditic [male and female on same plants]) woody, herbaceous annual that uses the sun more efficiently than virtually any other plant on our planet, reaching a robust 12 to 20 feet or more in one short growing season. It can be grown in virtually any climate or soil condition on Earth; even marginal ones. Each acre of hemp would yield 1000 gallons of methanol. Hemp fuel derivatives, along with the recycling of paper, etc., would be enough to run America virtually without oil.

About 6% of the contiguous United States land area put into cultivation for biomass could supply all current demands for oil and gas. It is a shame to all of us, that today, we will pay our farmers for not farming their land while we spend tens of billions of dollars every year to buy foreign oil. Acid rain, global warming, air and water pollution of all kinds result primarily from the use of fossil fuels.

In about 10 years, when our petroleum resources have dwindled to 20% of their original size. America will have four choices:

1. Burn all our poisonous coal;
2. Go to war over foreign oil; (we already have witnessed a small Persian Gulf Oil War)
3. Cut down our forest for fuel; or
4. Grow and process a variety of environmentally safe fuels for biomass.

The energy companies own most of the petro-chemicals, pharmaceutical, liquor, and tobacco companies, and are intertwined with insurance companies and banks. (U.S. companies are pushing the urine testing for marijuana.)

Many politicians now in power, according to the press, are bought and paid for by the energy companies, and their U.S. gov't arm is the CIA. (The Company- Robert Ludlum, etc.) The Bush/Quayle administration was uniquely tied to oil, newspapers, pharmaceuticals – and the CIA.

In 1910, South Africa began outlawing marijuana "to stop insolent Blacks!" And South Africa, along with Egypt, led the international (League of Nations: today the United Nations) fight to have cannabis outlawed worldwide.

History has shown the marijuana laws to be based on lies, prejudice, and greed. It is an international conspiracy of false religion, politics, and commerce.

"In later times, some shall... speak lies in hypocrisy... commanding to abstain from that which God hath created to be received with thanksgiving of them which believe and know the truth!" Paul: 1 Tim. 4:2-3

CHAPTER 29
"INTRODUCTION TO THE GREAT AMERICAN HEMP INDUSTRY"

By Jack Frazier

Civilizations are built on the efficient use of natural and human resources, and, to the extent they are truly civilized, they use these resources in a logical, humane way.

American society is in decline and on the verge of collapse because a small group of extremely wealthy and ignorant but clever males were allowed to gain control of virtually all natural resources, and now most human resources as well.

Up until the mid-thirties, this society used our resources in a somewhat logical and efficient way. Conservation still had meaning. The wholesale rape squandering of our resources was in its infancy. The so-called "great" corporations that now control every important political and economic decision still had a human dimension at that time.

Now, DuPont, Union Carbide, IBM, Chase Manhattan Bank, Exxon, et al, have become huge monsters that crush and mutilate everything and everyone that crosses their path or stands in their way. As the saying goes, power corrupts and absolute power corrupts absolutely.

There can be no logical use of natural resources as long as these human dinosaurs trample every logical proposal for a rational, natural lifestyle. A sustainable, long-range strategy to give society a humane dimension is what they fear most. Energy conservation and the legalization of hemp farming terrify them.

In spite of the above reality, many courageous members of our society continue to wage the seemingly hopeless struggle to bring meaning and logic to this "age of banditry now coming to a disastrous close." (Albert Howard)

For those of us who need some signs of hope – just to go on living, there are indeed a few hopeful signs on the horizon.

About ten percent of poor and middle-class people are, by choice, leading a rational, natural lifestyle. Some are remnants of early Native American cultures that never bought into our plastic society.

Others have a land-based ethic that sustains them and protects them from being subverted and seduced into abandoning their superior lifestyle. Still others have tried the plastic lifestyle and found it shallow, narrow- minded, selfish and cruel.

Sometimes periods of crisis, such as the one we're going through now, bring people to their senses and bring them together. Maybe that will happen in the 90s as it did for a short time in the 1960s and early 70s. If not, then "it's all over now baby blue." (Bob Dylan)

As this book and Herer's *The Emperor Wears No Clothes* shows, hemp has a role to play, repairing the damage done by the earth-rapists. It can provide the agricultural basis for a transition from plastics and fossil fuels to alternative fuels as no other agricultural crop can.

It played that role for thousands of years in dozens of civilizations going back to the very dawn of recorded history. In fact, if it hadn't been for hemp and the durable paper it provides, there would be no early recorded history. The inferior books and documents made from wood-pulp paper will barely last 50 years before deteriorating and falling apart. Hemp is both durable and strong. And as Jack Herer says, hemp can save the world - if we will let it.

West Virginians are not known for our ability to suffer injustice quietly. Maybe, some day "King George" Bush and others will learn what "Montani Semper Liberi" means. We didn't break away from the slavocracy to be re-enslaved by the New World Order, and monopoly business practices.

Jack Frazier, November 1991

West Virginia, U.S.A.

> *"It is a big idea: a new world order, where diverse nations are drawn together in common cause to achieve the universal aspirations of mankind: peace, and security, freedom and the rule of law... only the United States has both the moral standing and the means to back it up."*
> **Pres. George Bush, in his State of the Union address, Los Angeles Times, Feb. 18, 1991.**

The U.S. may have the means to back it up but it sure doesn't have the moral standing to create a new world order. Just recently, in June of 1992, Bush and the courts both showed their lack of moral.

Bush was the only World Leader at the Environmental Earth Summit in Brazil to refuse to ratify the bio-diversity agreement to protect the different plants and animals, saying it would cost U.S. companies.

Shortly after that, the Supreme Court ruled that it was O.K. to kidnap suspected law breakers from other countries, in violation of international law.

Might is not right — Right is Might

Leading statesmen and religious leaders are proposing a New World Order, a plan that many sincerely believe can bring peace on earth. Could it be that they are forging, not a New World Order, but rather the One World Order of apocalyptic prophecy?

CHAPTER 30
"THY KINGDOM COME OH JAH, THY RULE OH NEGUS I"

Before the Kingdom of God is to be established here on earth, certain things must come to pass. Scripture makes it abundantly clear that Babylon the Great is to fall. Babylon is revealed in the book of Revelations to be a three-headed beast composed of religion, politics, and commerce. Christ also exposed the hypocritical religious, political and commercial leaders.

It is only fitting that these leaders are supposed to be looking out for the flock — the masses of humanity. If the churches were of a truly spiritual nature, and the politicians truly cared about the people and if the corporate conglomerates were truly responsible members of society, then humanity would be in a position for solving its problems. This is not the case – when the head of the stream is corrupt, the whole stream becomes corrupt.

The book of Revelations reveals that the church became a whore with many like daughters. It became a whore in essence, because it went to bed with political and economic leaders. History has shown this to be the case with the Roman Catholic Church.

Historians indicate that for the first 300 to 400 years A.D., Christian sects were gentle and loving, open, tolerant and unstructured: a poor man's or slave's religion. This was until Roman Emperor Constantine feigned conversion to Christianity and set up the Roman Catholic Church. This became the official religion of the empire and anyone who didn't agree was persecuted.

In a series of councils, all contrary dogmas were outlawed and driven underground during the Dark Ages 400-900 A.D. All European people were forced to adhere to "Holy" Roman Empire policy with blind faith, and unquestioned version of how to worship God... and the Popes infallibility. Political rulers and merchants aided and abetted this fraud.

During this time, the people were forbidden to learn to read or write and often were punished or put to death for doing so.

The Scriptural ordinance of the Lord's Supper was supplanted by the idolatrous sacrifice of the mass. Papist priests pretended, by their senseless mummery, to convert the simple bread and wine into the actual "body and blood" of Christ. With blasphemous presumption, they openly claimed the power of creating God, the

Creator of all things. All Christians were required, on pain of death, to avow their faith in this horrible, heaven-insulting heresy. Multitudes who refused were given to the flames.

Still another fabrication was needed to enable Rome to profit by the fears and vices of her adherents. This was supplied by the doctrine of indulgences. Full remission of sins – past, present, and future; and release from all the pains and penalties incurred, were promised to those who would enlist in the pontiff's wars to extend his temporal dominion, to punish his enemies, or to exterminate those who dared deny his spiritual supremacy. The people were taught that by the payment of money to the church they might free themselves from sin, and release the souls of their deceased friends who were confined in the tormenting flames. By such means, Rome filled her coffers and sustained the magnificence, luxury, and vice of the pretended representatives of who had nowhere to lay *His* head.

In the Thirteenth Century was established that most terrible of all the engines of the Papacy - the Inquisition. The prince of darkness worked through the leaders of the papal hierarchy. In their secret councils, Satan and his angels controlled the minds of evil men, who invented tortures too horrible to appear to human eyes. "Babylon the Great" was drunken with the blood of the saints. The mangled forms of millions of martyrs cried to God for vengeance upon that apostate power.

While embracing wine as a sacrament, the Inquisition outlawed cannabis ingestion in Spain in the 12th century and France in the 13th. Anyone using hemp to communicate, heal, or otherwise was labeled a "witch." In 1484, Pope Innocent VIII proclaimed hemp, an unholy sacrament, of the second and third types of satanic mass, which lasted more than 150 years.

On July 18, 1870, a man who called himself Pope Pius IX told a big lie and said no Pope could ever make a mistake or commit a sin. He deceitfully spoke, saying: from that day on, every Pope was "infallible" - anything that a Pope said (or had already said) was law.

On Aug. 9, 1980 - In Castel Gandolfo, Italy, Pope John Paul spoke on Saturday, and said he was against marijuana "with all his soul."

This shows that the Roman Catholic Church is still in bed with economic and political leaders. This is the reason that during prohibition, they allowed the usage of wine as a sacrament, even though the Bible says, Proverb 20 v. 1 – "Wine is a mocker; strong drink is raging: and whosoever is deceived thereby is not wise."

Oct. 28, 1919, Washington, D.C. — "No one shall manufacture, sell, purchase, transport or prescribe any wine or liquor — this law does not apply to the manufacture, sale, transportation, importation, possession or distribution of wine for religious ritual."

A recent directive from higher Catholic authorities has authorized drinking of wine in church services. The Catholic Church claims that their Christian Brothers Wine is the blood of Christ, and is the Sacrament instituted at the last supper, when Christ said: "Partake of this freely, and do it in remembrance of me."

The Scribes and Pharisees wanted to know: "How can we eat of this man's flesh and drink his blood?"

To this day, the Catholics claim that this is a mystery which we can never understand, being "merely human."

Was it the sacrament which the Apostles partook so freely of, the wine that is served today in the Catholic Church? Could a man, by drinking wine continuously, draw closer to God?

The history of smoking marijuana as a sacrament is thousands of years old. The Pope's ritual of drinking wine is not even two hundred years old. (Insert list of acts by Catholic Church)

Because of the corrupt nature of the Catholic Church, the Protestant Reformation came into being. Martin Luther nailed to his church door the '95' Theses, which exposed the darkness and tyranny of the Roman Church and touched off the Reformation in Germany. The church was full of superstition, image worship, and empty ritual. Anyone labeled a heretic was burned alive.

The church was in the business of saving souls by an endless course of sacrifices of the mass; (as interpreted by the Catholic Church) ritual and penances money had to be paid for forgiveness. In order to retain power, bible reading individuals were martyred, books were burned, and the Catholic clergy were made to conform.

Because the Protestants were breaking off from a corrupt source, they too were lacking, especially from the standpoint of biblical understanding. The biggest falsehood perpetrated by Christendom is the concept of a Sky God, an unknown God, and a God separated from mankind. This is completely contrary to the teachings of Christ and the Bible. The Bible speaks against idols and idolatry, and that is exactly what was embraced. Man was pointed to pictures, crosses, statues, walls, rocks, relics, and Sky Gods. In the name of religion there has been war, torture, slavery, prejudice, oppression etc. God is not the author of this confusion.

In rejecting the truth, men reject its Author. In trampling upon the law of God, they deny the authority of the lawgiver. It is easy to make an idol of wood or stone. With many, the idol of philosophy is enthroned, while the living God, as revealed in His word, in Christ, and in the works of creation is worshipped by few.

No error accepted by Christendom strikes more boldly against the authority of Heaven, none is more directly opposed to the dictates of reason; none is more pernicious in its results, than the modern doctrine, so rapidly gaining ground that God's law is no longer binding upon men. Every nation has its laws, which command respect and obedience; no government could exist without them; and can it be conceived that the Creator of the heavens and earth has no law to govern the beings He has made?

In seeking to cast contempt upon the divine Statutes, Satan has perverted the doctrines of the Bible, and errors have been incorporated into the faith of thousands who profess to believe the Scriptures. The last great conflict between truth and error is but the final struggle of the long-standing controversy concerning the law of God. Upon this issue, we are now entering a battle between the laws of men and the precepts of God, between the religion of the Bible and the religion of fable and tradition.

Commerce has the people of the world doing anything and everything for money. The Bible says that the love of money is the root of all evil. When you oppress the next person or you destroy the environment or you sell your soul for money, God is not pleased. God is not pleased with the big corporations and the rich men who gained their riches by oppressing the poor and ruining the earth. Remember, great crime calls for great punishment.

God wants the rich to help uplift the poor and needy. The rich nations of the earth have a responsibility to help the Third World countries. In most cases, it was these same rich nations that contributed to Third World poverty through colonialism, slavery, and exploitation. These rich nations should remember that Justice and Judgment are the habitations of God's throne.

Mankind has to come to the realization that we are in fact in this together, that mankind is its brother's keeper — by the rich helping the less advantaged, we all will be better off. Mankind has the brains (if only the heart) to truly turn the earth into a Garden of Eden. Instead of destroying the earth more and more, we should be making it better and better.

Crime is the characterizing factor of this present age. When the rich commercial and political leaders are revealed to be a bunch of crooks, only interested in their own special interest, what can you expect from the poor masses struggling to survive.

It seems expedient at this time to make known our firm beliefs concerning the integrity and qualifications to be required of all people holding office of public trust, both secular and civil, as expounded by our great founding father of the Ethiopian Zion Coptic Church in Jamaica, Marcus Garvey.

CHAPTER 31
"GOVERNING THE IDEAL STATE BY MARCUS MOSIAH GARVEY NATIONAL HERO"

"Our modern systems of Government have partly failed and are wholly failing.

"We have tried various forms, but none has measured up to the **Ideal State**. Communism was the last attempt, and its most ardent advocates have acknowledged its limitations, shortcomings and impossibility.

"The reason for all this failure is not far to seek. The sum total of Government collapse is traceable to the growing spirit of selfishness, graft and greed within the individual. Naturally, the state cannot govern itself: it finds expression and executes its edicts through individuals, hence the State is human. Its animation is but the reflex of our human characters. As a Nero, Caesar, Alexander, Alfred, William, Louis, Charles, Cromwell, Washington, Lincoln, Roosevelt or Wilson thinks, so expresses the majesty of the State.

"If we must correct the maladministration of the State and apply the corporate majesty of the people to their own good, then we must reach the source and there reorganize or reform.

"Under the pressure of our civilization, with its manifold demands, the individual is tempted, beyond measure, to do evil or harm to others; and, if responsible, to the entire State and people. If by thus acting, he himself profits and those around him, there arises corruption in government, as well as in other branches of the secular and civil life ("a little leaven...").

"All other methods of Government having been tried and failed, I suggest a reformation that would place a greater responsibility upon the shoulders of the elect and force them either to be the criminals that some of us believe they are, or the good and true representatives we desire them to be.

"Government should be absolute, and the head should be thoroughly responsible for himself and the acts of his subordinates.

"When we elect a President of a nation, he should be endowed with absolute authority to appoint all his lieutenants from cabinet ministers, Governors of States and territories, administrators and judges to minor officers. He should swear his life as a guarantee to the State and people, and he should be made to pay the price of such a life if he deceives, grafts, bows to special privilege or interest, or in any way undermines the sacred honor and trust imposed upon him by acts of favoritism, injustice or friendly or self-interests. He should be the soul of honor, and when he is legally or properly found to the contrary, he should be publicly disgraced, and put to death as an outcast and an unworthy representative of the righteous will of the people.

"A President should, by proper provisions made by the State, be removed from all pecuniary obligations and desires of a material nature. He should be voted a salary and other accommodations so large and sufficient as to make it reasonably impossible for him, or those dependent upon him, to desire more during his administration. He and his family should be permanently and substantially provided for after the close of his administration, and all this and possibly more should be done for the **purpose of removing him from the slightest possible material temptations or want.** He, in turn, should devote his entire time to the sovereign needs and desires of the people. He should, for all the period of his administration, remove himself from obligatory, direct and fraternal contact with any and all special friends. His only friends outside of his immediate family should be the State. He should exact by law from all his responsible and administrative appointees a similar obligation, and he should enforce the law by penalty of death.

"His administrators and judges should be held to strict accountability, and on the committing of any act of injustice, unfairness, favoritism or malfeasance, should be taken before the public, disgraced and then stoned to death, (This is the ancient penalty called for in Leviticus 20 of the King James edition of the Holy Bible for those wizards who cause the people to be defiled.)

"This system would tend to attract, to the sacred function of Government and judicial administration, only men and women of the highest and best characters, whom the public would learn to honor and respect with such satisfaction as to obliterate and prevent the factional party fights of Socialism, Communism, Anarchism, etc., for the control of Government, because of the belief that Government is controlled in the interest of classes, and not for the good of all the people. It would also discourage the self-seekers, grafters, demagogues and charlatans from seeking public offices, as the penalty of discovery of crime would be public disgrace and death for them and their families.

"The state should hold the wife of a President, and the wives of all administrative officials, solely responsible for their domestic households, and they should be required by law to keep a strict and accurate public account of all receipts and disbursements of their husbands during their administrative terms; and if any revenue comes into the household other than provided by law, should be promptly reported to the responsible officer of the State for immediate action; and should the wife conceal or refuse to make such a disclosure, and that it be discovered afterwards, and it was an act of crime against the dignity and high office of the incumbent, she and her husband should be publicly disgraced and put to death. But any child or member of the family, who before discovery, reports the act, should be spared the disgrace and publicly honored by the populace for performing a duty to the State.

"The State should require that the husband and his consort, under the severest penalty for non-performance, report the full amount of his entire wealth to the State before taking office, and that all incomes and salaries legally authorized be reported promptly to the wife to enable her to keep a proper public account.

"Whenever a President or high official, during his term, has performed solemnly and truly all his duties to the people and State, and he is about to retire, he should be publicly proclaimed and honored by the populace, and all during his life he and his family should occupy a special place of honor and respect among the people. They should be respected by all with whom they come in contact, and at death they should be granted public funerals and their names added to the niche in the Hall of Fame of the Nation. Their names should be placed on the Honor Roll of the Nation, and their deeds of righteousness should be handed down to the succeeding generations of the race, and their memories sung by the poets of the nation.

"For those who have abused their trusts, images of them should be made and placed in a national hall of criminology and ill fame, and their crimes should be recited and a curse pronounced upon them and their generations.

"Governments left to the free and wanton will and caprice of the individual in an age so corrupt as this, without any vital reprimand or punishment for malfeasance, other than ordinary imprisonment, will continue to produce dissatisfaction, and cause counter agitations of a dangerous nature, and upheavals destructive to the good of society and baneful to the higher hopes and desires of the human race.

"This plan I offer to the race as a means to which we may perfect the establishment of a new system of Government, conducive to the best interest of the people and a blessing to our disorganized society of the twentieth century."

THE ETHIOPIAN ZION COPTIC CHURCH

We of the Ethiopian Zion Coptic Church know ourselves to be the fathers of our race. The officers and members of our Church are required to be above the reproach of God and man. Our desire and aim is the improvement of mankind through the perfect example of Christ our Father, and the establishment on earth of God's Moral Law.

Men's self-willed government has failed. The Ethiopian Zion Coptic Church stands up as a light in this time of doubt and sorrow, to lead a troubled world to a home of peace and safety.

Psalms 141: 2 *"Let my prayer be set forth before Thee as incense; and the lifting up of my hands as the evening sacrifice."*

Daniel 7: 13-14 *"I saw in the night visions, and behold, one like the Son of man came with the clouds of heaven, and came to the Ancient of days, and they brought him near before him. ¹⁴ And there was given him dominion, and glory, and a kingdom, that all people, nations, and languages should serve him: his dominion is an everlasting dominion, which shall not pass away, and his kingdom which shall be not destroyed."*

Marijuana wasn't against the law at the time the Constitution was written. The Founding Fathers would surely be displeased with the war against the marijuana culture.

COPTIC COURT CASES

Note the following findings concerning the Ethiopian Zion Coptic Church:

Judge Frederich Barad, Dade County Circuit Court, Miami, Florida - U.S.A. January 17, 1979:

"The Ethiopian Zion Coptic Church represents a religion within the meaning of the First Amendment to the Constitution of the United States.

"Regarding the nature of the religious beliefs and practices of the Ethiopian Zion Coptic Church pertinent to the instant litigation, this Court finds the following:

"a. Cannabis is not itself an object of worship. Rather, prayer is directed solely to a spiritual 'God.'

"b. Cannabis is smoked as the mystical body and blood of 'Jes-us,' serves to permit a member of the faith to go deeper within his consciousness to see everything that he has done wrong; serves to permit a member to find a spirit of love, unity and justice within himself so as to enable that member to convey such to others; serves to open a members morale equilibrium, to plant the seed of unfaltering righteousness, and to allow a member to see and know that 'God' is a man; serves to bring a member closer to 'God' and to the divine communication of 'the living God,' and serves as a remembrance of 'God.'

"h. The use of cannabis is an essential portion of the religious practice."

Florida Supreme Court, November 1, 1979:

"The Ethiopian Zion Coptic Church is not a new church or religion — but the record reflects it is centuries old and has regularly used cannabis (ganja) as its sacrament.

"Bona fide members who are adults have a right to worship in the manner that the Coptic Church has done for centuries — before the adoption of the United States Constitution or the discovery of America."

Two excellent reviews have recently been written concerning a church case against the D.E.A., asking for a marijuana exemption similar to the one giving the Native American Indians the right to use peyote in their religious services. Peyote, like marijuana, remains in schedule I substances, meaning the substance has a high potential for abuse, has no medical use, and is not safe under medical supervision. Although marijuana remains in Schedule 1, it definitely belongs in a less restrictive category.

The two excellent reviews are, *Marijuana as a Holy Sacrament*, by Cindy Mazur, Vol. 5, Notre Dame Journal of Law, Ethics and Public Policy, No 3 (1991), page 693; and *Accommodating Religious Drug Use and Society's War on Drugs*, by Lesley Frank, VOL 58, George Washington Law Review, page 1019 (June 1990).

NOTRE DAME JOURNAL OF LAW, ETHICS AND PUBLIC POLICY [Vol.5]: MARIJUANA AS A "HOLY SACRAMENT"

V. Conclusion

Congress and the DEA have accorded a sacramental drug exemption to Native Americans regarding peyote. The EZCC (Ethiopian Zion Coptic Church) has tried for years to obtain a similar exemption regarding marijuana. This past June, the Supreme Court denied certiorari to the District of Columbia Court of Appeals decision denying the EZCC a sacramental drug exemption similar to that held by the NAC.

The D.C. Court of Appeals decision to deny an exemption to the EZCC violates the establishment clause of the U.S. Constitution. This court's reliance on the DEA's statement that it has greater law enforcement control problems with marijuana will not satisfy an application of strict scrutiny. The DEA must explain why a very narrow exemption extended to one-hundred to two-hundred people would undermine its interest in preventing drug abuse, when an unlimited exemption for peyote extended to 300,000 to 400,000 people does not. Additionally, there must be a forthright analysis of the current trends regarding the public's abuse of marijuana and the growing body of information concerning marijuana's use for medicinal purposes.

The appeals court set forth various aspects of the NAC (Native American Church) which made it particularly well suited for an exemption; then failed to recognize that the EZCC has demonstrated significant similarity to the NAC regarding these aspects. For example, the EZCC views the recreational use of its sacrament as sacrilegious, has much stricter controls on its membership, and regards marijuana as a deity as does the NAC concerning peyote. Additionally, as a result of its proposed exemption, the EZCC would exercise much greater control over its ceremony than the NAC.

The EZCC is being denied a benefit accorded to another church because of its ritual; its traditions because it is not indigenous, and because of the abuse of its sacrament by non-members. The EZCC has proposed to modify its tradition and ritual, to adhere to practices which are much more restrictive than those of the NAC, and to help with monitoring problems, to no avail.

The reasons for the denial appear to flow from the fact that the EZCC is a relatively new religion to this country, of black origin, small and unpopular. The establishment clause was specifically written to protect these very types of religions from being denied benefits extended to more politically popular religious groups. If the EZCC were accorded basic protections guaranteed by establishment clause, its right to partake of marijuana as its holy sacrament, in accordance with its narrow exemption proposed by Olsen, could not be denied.

Even with these findings in the lower Courts, the U.S. Federal Courts have consistently ruled that the Ethiopian Zion Coptic Church has no right to its sacrament and that governmental interest outweighs any FIRST AMENDMENT RIGHTS the Church has.

A recent First Amendment decision by the Supreme Court now maintains that religious liberty is a "luxury" that government is free to ignore. Freedom of Religion was such an important concept in early America that it was incorporated in the First Amendment of the Constitution; school children were and still are taught that the Pilgrims fled Europe in order to find religious freedom in America.

At the same time, the government very reluctantly is supplying government-grown marijuana to glaucoma and cancer patients. Ten states have decriminalized up to an ounce and up until recently, one could grow a few plants in the state of Alaska.

The government acknowledges that marijuana is essential to the faith of the Ethiopian Zion Coptic Church. (It is "The Body and Blood," the sacrament of the Church). It is the Biblical "Tree of Life," for the healing of the nations.

We believe that to outlaw the Church's sacrament is to fight against God's Saints and the setting up of God's peaceful Kingdom here on earth. We seek to build a Kingdom of Peace, of Brotherly Love, an uncompetitive world in which we help one another; in which the weapons of mass destruction are turned into plowshares... a truly "United Nations" in which all nations, kindreds and peoples bow to Gods Universal Moral Law.

This is prophesied in the Bible and we owe it to our children and their children to usher in this truly spiritual and enlightened Age. Each and every one of us has to write the commandments of God in our hearts, so that everyone will know God and will be worthy to partake of the Biblical "Tree of Life."

CHAPTER 32
"THE GOD-MAN AND REVELATION OF JESUS"

Philippians 2:5-6 — *"Let this mind be in you, which was also in Christ Jesus; who, being in the form of God, thought it not robbery to be equal with God."*

The God-Man is a very important concept: the concept of the God in Man or the living God, as opposed the God outside of man — the sky God or unknown God. Jesus said to the multitudes "Know ye not that you are the temple of God"... "Know ye not that ye are Gods?"

Matthew 1: 23 – *"They shall call his name Emmanuel, which being interpreted is, God with us."*

Jes-us is by interpretation JUST-US, the collective body of Christ (many members and one body) as opposed to worshipping one man. For Christ was trying to enlighten all mankind. He was the Logos, Jes-us Christ, the DIVINE WORD.

St. John 1:1 – *"In the beginning was the WORD, and the WORD was with God, and the WORD God."*

St. John 1:12-14 – *"But as many as received him, to them gave he power to become the sons of God, even to them that believe on his name. [13]Which were born, not of blood, nor of the will of the flesh, nor of the will of man, but of God. [14]And the WORD was made flesh, and dwelt among us, (and we beheld his glory, the glory as of the only begotten of the Father), full of grace and truth."*

Revelation 21:7 – *"He that overcometh shall inherit all things; and I will be his God, and he shall be my son."*

So you see that Christ was a prototype. He was the first fruit of many to come, Truly God and truly man. God incarnate, man divine, Thy word is true; for man will not live by bread alone, but by every WORD that proceedeth out of the mouth of God.

Taken from *Gandhi, Soldier of Nonviolence*, by Calvin Kytle:

Mohandas K. Gandhi, one of the greatest leaders in the history of India and a student of religion could not accept the idea that Jesus was the only incarnate son of God "If God could have sons, all of us were his sons," he said on a close examination of the Bible, it is revealed that in fact anyone who walks in the word of God is worthy to be called a Son.

Violence, Gandhi decided irrevocably, was an insult to God's intent for man.

Gandhi came to equate life with time and to see the acceptance of death as a condition of freedom. A man's achievements in life, he reasoned, were nothing more than the constructive uses he made of his time on earth; the freedom to work for the common welfare, to embrace poverty, to find truth.

It was plain that for a man to be free, and therefore free to make the most of his time, he first had to conquer his fear of death. And how best to conquer the fear of death? – By believing in something so strongly he is willing to die for it.

Christ also came to this conclusion.

Gandhi's strategy was nonviolent resistance to unjust laws, carried out by the masses sworn to God, and psychologically prepared imprisonment or death. Gandhi's organization's members were known as the warriors of truth and love.

Gandhi's understanding allowed him to see beyond the world of chaos into a universe of order; to stay in an insane society; to live inwardly at peace in the midst of pain and injustice; to fight the sickness in mankind without becoming sickened. In one of Gandhi's speeches he said:

"Truth is the end; love a means there to... The Golden Rule is to dare to do the right at any cost."

Gandhi was fighting a religious battle in an attempt to revolutionize the political outlook.

Some argue that Gandhi was ahead of his time, and his ideas have more relevance for the future than during his lifetime.

Gandhi's most important contribution was to our understanding of ourselves and particularly of our potential for personal growth. For what Gandhi did, most of all was to give us a new vision of man.

"Nonviolence is the law of our species," he maintained, and he lived his life to prove that it could be. Most particularly, he demonstrated man's capacity to change. In a technological age where change is likely to be equated with survival, the lesson could be crucial. There are political theorists who, since Gandhi's death, have come to see non-violence as the only realistic alternative to nuclear warfare and global annihilation.

The following are excerpts from the Allen Burke talk show that is syndicated nationally in the U.S. (if not internationally). The brother is a spokesman:

Bro.: "*The book of Hosea, chapter four, the first two verses. Hear the word of the Lord ye children of Israel. For the Lord has a controversy with the inhabitants of the land because there is no truth, nor mercy, nor knowledge of God in the land. By swearing and lying and killing and stealing and committing adultery, they break out, and blood touches blood (for the rules of right, the commission of man's deeds, the consequences resulting there from).*"

Burke: "*That was obviously written about the congress of the United States. (There is chuckling).*"

Bro.: "*Completely accurate again. It's about the U.S., about Jamaica, the land they call Israel, England, Australia, etc, all because the world today has become full of swearing, lying, stealing the committing of adultery.*"

Further along it is continued:

Bro.: "*The history of this Church goes back thousands of years, and there has been a marked point of breaking off between this Church and the known religions of the world, and that has to do with the nature of Christ. The religions of the world, the popes and Billy Grahams talk about a Christ with two natures, one of earth and one up in the sky or heaven, wherever that's supposed to be. We today and always have talked about the Godman. Not God and man, yet the Godman. That every man has a responsibility to, not just to be aware of that Christian, fundamental doctrine, but to live it and apply it to our lives.*

"*It looks like nowadays the people are looking for a spiritual understanding of life. Our generation is coming of age, not only the ones in the church, but overall. We have to decide now whether to adopt and continue what's been set before us, which would include military, politics, drugs, fertilizers, chemicals; a corrupt, polluted earth; or whether we are going to accept the wisdom of ages, which is very different from what you see in America today."*

CHAPTER 33
"MAN AN ANGEL"

Revelation 22:8-9 – "*And I John saw these things, and heard them. And when I had heard and seen, I fell down to worship before the feet of the angel which shewed me these things. ⁹Then he saith unto me, See thou do it not: for I am my fellow-servant, and of thy brethren the prophets, and of them which keep the sayings of this book: worship God.*"

SOURCES

Richard E. Schultes, article: "Man and Marijuana"

Richard E. Schultes and Albert Hofmann, *Plants of the Gods—Origin of Hallucinogenic Use* (McGraw-Hil Book co. LUK.) Limited, England, 1979)

G.S. Chopra, article: "Man and Marijuana," International Journal of the Addict, 1969, 4, 215-247.

Ernest L. Abel, Marijuana, the First Twelve Thousand Years (Phenum Press, New York, 1980)

Ernest L. Abel, A *Comprehensive Guide to Cannabis Literature*

Ernest L. Abel, Marijuana Dictionary: Words, Terms, Events Persons Relating to Cannabis (Greenwood press, Westpoint, Connecticut (19821)

Edward M. Brecher and the Editors of *Consumer Reports, The Consumer Union Report*, "Licit and Illicit Drugs", (Little, Brown, and CO.)

Lewin L, Phantastica, Narcotic and Stimulating Drugs: Their Use and Abuse, (London: Kegan, Trench, Turbner, and co., Ltd. Translated from the second German edition by PHA 1931) (N.Y., Dutton, 1964, reprint, 1924, trans. 1931)

Sula Benet, *Cannabis and Culture*, ed. V. Rubin (The Hague: Moutan, 1975)

Richard E. Lingeman, *Drugs From A to Z, A Dictionary* (McGraw-Hill Book Co., 1969, 74)

John R. Glowa, *The Encyclopedia of Psychoactive Drugs* (Chelsea House Pub., N.Y., New Haven, Philadelphia, 1986)

George Andrew and Simon Vinkenoog, *The Book of Grass: An Anthology on Indian Hemp*; Chandler and Sharp Series in Cross Culture Themes (N.Y., Grove press (19671)

Jack Herer, *The Emperor Wears No Clothes or Anything You Ever Wanted to Know About Marijuana*, 1985.
Barbara Makeda Levi, Rastafari - The New Creation, (Jamaica Media Productions Ltd. 1981)

Peter J. Furst, *Hallucinogens and Culture* (Chandler and Sharp Publishers, Inc., 1976)

Baudelaire, Artificial Paradises

Dr. Charles Tart, *On Being Stoned: A Psychological Study of Marijuana Intoxication* (Science and Behavior, 1971)

William A. Emboden, Jr., *Ritual Use of Cannabis Sativa L*

S.I. Rudenko, *Frozen Tombs of Siberia* (Dent., London, 1970)

Edward Atchley, *A History of the Use of Incense in Divine Worship*

E.A. Wallis Budge, *The Divine Origin of the Craft of the Herbalist*

Egon Corti, *A History of Smoking, by Count Corti*; Translated by Paul England (G. G. Harrap, London, England, 1931)

Francis Robicsek, *The Smoking Gods: Tobacco in Mayan Art, History and Religion* (University of Oklahoma Press, Norman, 1978)

Diodorus, *Histories* 1.97.7

Vera Rubin and Lambros Comitas Ganja in Jamaica (The Hague, Paris 1975)

Hermann Schneider, *History of World Civilization*, 2v (New York, 1931)

M.N. Dhalla, *Zoroastrian Civilization* (Oxford University Press, N.Y., 1922)

Sir Charles Eliot, Hinduism and Buddhism 3v. (Routledge & K. Paul, London 1921)

A.A. McDonnell, *India's Past* (The Clarendon Press, Oxford, 1927)

Charles Anthon, *A Classical Dictionary* (N.Y., Harpers and Brothers, 1848)

G. Maspero, *The Dawn Of Civilization: Egypt and Chaldea* (London, 1897)

Lucy Lamy, *Egyptian Mysteries*

Friedrich Ratzell, *History of Mankind* (N. Y Gordon press)

R.H. Charles, *The Book of Jubilees*, cap, iij, (London, 1902)

Alfred Wiedemann, *Religion of the Ancient Egyptians* (London, 1897)

Geoffrey Wainwright, *Eucharist and Eschatology* (Epworth Press, London, 1971)

Webster's Third New International Dictionary, 1966.

The Book of the Dead, Edit. E.A.W. Budge, British Museum, 1895, p. 250

J. Jermias, in Encyclopedia IV, 4119, quoting Rawlinson, Cuneiform Inscription IV. 19 (59) Cnf. the story of Bel and the Dragon.

John McKenzie, *The Bible Dictionary* (N.Y. MacMillan pub. co., 1965)

Encyclopedia Britannica, *"Holy Spirit"* (15th Edition, 1978) Micropaedia, Ready Reference and Index

Encyclopedia Britannica, *"Sacrifice"* (15th Edition, 1978)

Encyclopedia Britannica, *"Pharmacological Cults"* (15th Edition, 1978), p. 199

Encyclopedia Britannica, "Coptic"

Encyclopedia Britannica, "Essenes"

Encyclopedia Britannica, "Theraputea"

Encyclopedia Britannica, "Sacred Pipe" (15th Edition)

Encyclopedia Britannica, "Incense"

Encyclopedia Britannica, "Hemp" (Micropaedia Ready Reference and Index, p. 1016)

Encyclopedia Britannica, "Roman Catholicism, The Eucharist" (Volume 15, p. 998)

Encyclopedia Britannica, "Mysticism"

King James Version of the Bible

The Apocrypha

"FINAL WORDS"

We hope you enjoyed this information. If you have any question or comments, we would like to see them. Send them to the Ethiopian Zion Coptic Church.

We of the Ethiopian Zion Coptic Church decided to publish this in order to give the public an opportunity to study the church and its doctrine; not from inflated and misleading media, but from historical and Biblical references. The Church has received extensive publicity through various mediums: *60 Minutes* has done a segment; *Life, Omni, Science, Rolling Stone, and High Times* magazines have all done articles; countless newspaper articles have been written, and various brothers have been on radio and TV talk shows around the country. We of the Ethiopian Zion Coptic Church revere ganja (marijuana) as our "holy" Eucharist and "spiritual intensifier" with Biblical, historical and divine associations for its use. Ganja is the mystical body and blood of "Jes-us" – burnt offering made by fire—which allows a member to see and know the "living God," or the "God in man." This is the greatest fulfillment that one can find— which is ultimate peace.

"About The Author"

Jeff Brown, the main researcher and organizer of this book, grew up in Miami, Florida in a middle class family. He heard about and joined the Ethiopian Zion Coptic Church in 1975 at the age of 19. Like many young Americans he was an experienced marijuana user and had witnessed many governmental lies about marijuana. In 1980 Jeff served 5 years in federal prison for violating various U.S. laws prohibiting his sacrament. While incarcerated he did most of the research for his book. His incarceration only reaffirmed his beliefs that marijuana is undoubtedly one of God's greatest gifts to mankind and that any law against it, is only political mischief.

Jeff Brown has travelled extensively throughout the Caribbean, North America and Europe advocating the legalization of ganja, without fear or favour. He is presently domiciled in the hills of Jamaica where he plants his own food etc.

Jeff would like to see an International Action in the World Court Convention Treaty in regards to marijuana prohibition. He would like to see the treaty challenged on religious, cultural, medicinal and commercial grounds.

For those interested in this action or in the Church Jeff can be written at:-

Coptic Farm
Creighton Hall
White Horses
St. Thomas
Jamaica

Or

P.O. Box 1161
Minneola, Florida
34755-1161
U.S.A.

INDEX

Africa, 3, 4, 13, 14, 16, 17, 29, 33, 35, 38, 42, 90, 93, 102, 126, 136
African, 9, 16, 91, 93, 94
Ancient Egyptians, 16, 95, 96
Ancient Kemet, 3, 4

Bible, 11, 38, 45, 47, 48, 49, 50, 54, 57, 60, 63, 72, 94, 95, 96, 106, 109, 126, 143, 144, 145, 147, 153, 155, 161, 162
Bowls, 34, 42

Cannabis, 3, 4, 5, 6, 7, 10, 13, 14, 15, 16, 17, 20, 21, 22, 23, 26, 27, 29, 30, 31, 36, 37, 40, 43, 44, 45, 48, 55, 59, 72, 76, 77, 81, 83, 99, 100, 102, 103, 104, 118, 119, 123, 124, 125, 127, 137, 142, 150, 159, 160
Caribbean, 4, 5, 6, 34, 131, 164
Ceremonial, 28, 34, 37, 42, 83, 86
Ceremonies, 16, 28, 36, 59
Chants, 11
Chillum pipe, 4
China, 4, 14, 26, 49, 63, 91, 100
Christ, 19, 43, 53, 54, 56, 57, 58, 59, 60, 61, 62, 63, 64, 65, 66, 67, 70, 72, 73, 74, 75, 76, 88, 92, 100, 101, 109, 111, 112, 113, 121, 141, 142, 143, 144, 149, 154, 155, 156
Communion, 5, 14, 47, 58, 64, 65, 67, 68, 69, 72, 74, 88, 98, 102, 107, 117, 121
Coptic Church, 11, 35, 38, 41, 57, 63, 66, 69, 77, 90, 102, 107, 108, 114, 121, 145, 149, 150, 151, 153 163, 164
Corinthians, 61, 62, 65, 67, 70
Culture, 33, 38, 46, 70, 84, 88, 93, 99, 149

Dagga, 9, 17

Egypt, 3, 4, 17, 33, 47, 57, 58, 60, 69, 91, 93, 100, 102, 118, 137, 161
Ethiopia, 16, 17, 35, 41, 53, 90
Ethiopian, 10, 12, 35, 38, 41, 63, 66, 67, 69, 77, 90, 93, 108, 109, 121, 145, 149, 150, 151, 152, 153, 163, 164
Europe, 4, 29, 30, 31, 91, 152, 164

Ganja, 3, 5, 6, 7, 9, 11, 13, 38, 39, 75, 106, 107, 108, 110, 112, 113, 114, 133, 160, 163
Garden of Eden, 16, 41, 90, 94, 145
Glaucoma, 40, 118, 124, 125, 152
Gnostic, 31, 59, 72, 75, 101
Gnosticism, 60
God, 11, 14, 20, 21, 23, 31, 36, 39, 41, 45, 47, 48, 50, 52, 54, 55, 56, 59, 60, 61, 62, 63, 64, 67, 68, 69, 70, 72, 75, 76, 84, 86, 90, 96, 97, 98, 99, 100, 101, 102, 103, 106, 107, 109, 110, 111, 112, 113, 114, 116, 117, 121, 126, 127, 137, 141, 142, 143, 144, 145, 149, 150, 153, 154, 155, 156, 157, 158, 163, 164

Hashish, 3, 4, 16, 41, 44, 68, 79, 133
Hebrew, 33, 34, 43, 44, 45, 64, 111

Hemp, 3, 13, 14, 16, 17, 18, 19, 20, 21, 22, 23, 24, 26, 27, 28, 29, 30, 31, 32, 35, 41, 43, 44, 45, 48, 56, 57, 59, 68, 73, 75, 83, 96, 97, 98, 99, 100, 103, 104, 120, 127, 129, 133, 134, 135, 136, 138, 139, 142
Herb, 3, 6, 7, 24, 29, 31, 35, 36, 38, 39, 55, 62, 72, 75, 96, 97, 117
Herbs, 9, 22, 31, 32, 39
Hindu, 5, 21, 23, 24, 52, 55, 56, 69, 75, 95, 99, 100
Holy Herb, 3, 4, 5, 6, 7, 39, 77
Holy Spirit, 56, 59, 63, 64, 67, 69, 73, 74, 76, 161
Holy Trinity, 4

Incense, 3, 5, 19, 26, 32, 41, 42, 43, 44, 45, 47, 48, 49, 50, 52, 53, 54, 59, 62, 63, 64, 66, 88, 90, 100, 112, 149
India, 4, 5, 14, 21, 23, 49, 52, 55, 75, 91, 100, 155, 161
Inspiration, 22, 62, 63, 74, 76, 81, 133

Jamaica, 4, 5, 6, 9, 10, 11, 12, 35, 38, 40, 65, 74, 101, 145, 156, 160, 164
Japan, 28, 49
Jesus, 38, 39, 53, 54, 57, 58, 59, 60, 64, 67, 72, 76, 77, 92, 101, 154, 155
Joints, 34

Kingston, 6, 40, 131
Kutche, 4

Marijuana, 3, 4, 5, 6, 7, 9, 11, 13, 14, 15, 16, 17, 18, 19, 21, 23, 24, 26, 27, 29, 32, 34, 35, 36, 37, 40, 42, 43, 44, 46, 49, 52, 55, 57, 58, 59, 62, 63, 65, 66, 67, 68, 69, 71, 72, 73, 74, 75, 77, 78, 81, 82, 83, 84, 85, 86, 87, 88, 89, 90, 95, 96, 99, 100, 101, 102, 103, 116-143, 149, 151, 153, 159, 160, 163, 164
Medicinal, 3, 11, 19, 22, 31, 40, 88, 100, 124, 133, 151, 164
Medicine, 17, 20, 26, 27, 30, 59, 60, 61, 118, 119, 124, 127, 129
Middle East, 14, 118
Moslems, 20, 22, 89
Mystical, 20, 38, 68, 74, 75, 150, 163

Pipes, 34
Psychotherapeutic, 82
Pygmies, 13, 17

Rastafari, 4, 5, 6, 7, 9, 39, 160
Relaxant, 77
Religions, 7, 13, 14, 48, 52, 56, 69, 70, 89, 95, 98, 100, 107, 152, 156
Roman Catholic Church, 31, 33, 57, 74, 97, 118, 127, 141, 143

Sacrament, 3, 4, 6, 7, 113, 143, 151
Sacramental, 5, 11, 58, 76, 78, 110, 151
Sanctification, 76
Scriptures, 25, 47
Semitic, 45, 46, 92, 93
Shiva, 21, 23, 25, 55, 56, 75, 95, 100
Smoking, 4, 5, 17, 32, 34, 35, 36, 38, 39, 47, 48, 54, 55, 59, 62, 63, 64, 65, 66, 77, 78, 85, 86, 87,

108, 122, 123, 128, 129, 131, 134, 143
Spirit, 14, 20, 23, 24, 28, 36, 39, 48, 53, 59, 62, 63, 64, 65, 70, 72, 73, 75, 76, 84, 88, 96, 110, 111, 114, 116, 117, 146, 150
Spiritual, 4, 7, 11, 14, 31, 38, 39, 52, 58, 59, 62, 63, 64, 65, 66, 67, 74, 75, 76, 78, 82, 96, 101, 117, 141, 142, 150, 153, 157, 163
Spliff, 4, 5

Steamer, 4

THC, 81, 83, 96, 99
Tobacco, 34, 35, 36, 66, 76, 125, 129, 131, 136
Traditional, 7, 28, 45, 85, 88, 125
Transfiguration, 53, 54, 95
Tree of Life, 11, 90

West Indies, 12, 38, 40